THE RUNNER STUMBLES

Night Rainbows

THE RUNNER STUMBLES

a play in two acts
&

Night Rainbows

an afterword
by

Milan Stitt

James T. White & Company
Clifton, New Jersey

For

T.A.L.

THE RUNNER STUMBLES was suggested by an actual turn-of-the-century trial for the murder of a nun in Michigan.

Time: April, 1911

Setting: A unit set, sparsely furnished, representing a cell, courtroom, and gravesite and, at various times during the action, other locations in Solon, Michigan.

NOTE: For this reading version, many lines which were cut for production purposes have been restored. What can be made clear by the presence of an actor is not necessarily clear on the printed page. The restorations made in this version of the play are for reading purposes only and should not be added to any actual stage presentations of the work as set forth in the Dramatists Play Service edition. For reading ease, Father Rivard is called Rivard in the present-tense scenes in the cell and courtroom. In past-tense scenes, when a memory has greater importance in his mind than the court proceedings, he is called Priest. In addition, the places in which his memories are acted out, such as his study and the front porch, are indicated at the beginning of the memories as a reading aid. These arbitrary divisions should not be interpreted as scenes; the events of the play follow rapidly upon each other without any scene breaks, often overlapping. Characters frequently remain frozen on stage when not involved in the scene on which Father Rivard's mind is focused. The controlling concept of focus is always in the mind of Father Rivard.

Act I

In the darkened theatre the mournful wail of a distant train whistle is heard, followed by the voice of the prosecutor at the arraignment: "Then may this matter of the People of the State of Michigan versus Brian Rivard be set down for immediate trial."

The lights come up on stage to reveal Father Rivard being led by the guard, Amos, to the cell.

Father Rivard would still be considered a young priest because of his actual age and boyish features, but he walks like an old man who trudges forward only because of the promise of death ahead. He does not wear a clerical collar.

Amos has no hopes, no dreams. Like most young men in Solon, his eyes brighten only at the prospect of cruelty. His eyes glisten now because of the little cruelties he and his friends have planned to play on Father Rivard.

Rivard is in a state that, exaggerated, would be catatonic. He just wants to be left alone. He wears handcuffs. Amos urges him forward, finally pushing Rivard in cell.

THE CELL

(Rivard looks up at cell window as he hears children singing "The Lilac Song")

AMOS: That's the children singing at the school, Father.

RIVARD: You hear it too?

AMOS: Ain't deaf, Father.

RIVARD: No. That's not what I— See, for a moment I thought . . . Sister Rita taught that song, but I couldn't possibly hear voices from up on the hill, could I?

AMOS: No. It's from the public school down here. There ain't been no Catholic school up there since you ran off.

(Amos sees Erna Prindle approaching the cell. She is plump and high-strung from her unnatural vulnerability. If she could cry upon seeing Father Rivard, it would be easier, but she doesn't want to. She wants to confess and then convince him of a maturity she has gained. If he believes it, maybe she can too.

Erna is looking back, making certain no one has seen her. She carries a napkin which holds muffins)

AMOS: Erna. What are you doing back here?

RIVARD: *(Surprised to see her)* Erna.

AMOS: You ain't ever supposed to come back here.

ERNA: I have to, Amos. I have to. You don't understand, Amos. Please. Leave me alone a minute.

(Amos remains)

I'll be all right. I will.

(Amos exits. Erna tentatively approaches cell)

RIVARD: Hello, Erna. Thank you for coming.

ERNA: *(Kneeling, crossing herself, ready for confession)* Father. Let me tell the truth right out. I haven't been to confesssion for four and a half years.

RIVARD: Erna. I can't.

ERNA: Of course you can, Father.

RIVARD: *(Taking Erna's arm to help her stand)* What's that, Erna? What do you have there?

ERNA: *(Handing him napkin)* For you. I made it up special. Your favorite. Do you remember what I always made for you?

RIVARD: Ice cream.

ERNA: Stop. You can see it's from the oven.

RIVARD: Pumpkin pie.

ERNA: Go on with you. You are just the same.

RIVARD: Mince meat muffins.

ERNA: Yes, yes. I knew you'd remember. I cook for the prisoners here. We live just up the road. The yellow house. Right in town now 'cause I'm married, Father. Maurice Prindle. He's thirty years older, but we have three children already. So it takes a lot, and I cook for them here.

RIVARD: That's good.

ERNA: Maurice isn't Catholic.

RIVARD: I remember.

ERNA: But it's wrong.

RIVARD: Marriage, if you're happy, if it does that, Erna, how can it be wrong?

ERNA: (*Confused, trying to think of something else*) If you look out your window, Father, you can see Holy Rosary Church up on the hill. I can see it from my kitchen. If you're troubled or scared, you can just stand and look at it. It's a comfort, a real comfort.

AMOS: (*As he enters*) You better get moving, Erna. His lawyer just came and is talking with the sheriff. Then he'll be coming back here.

ERNA: (*Frantic that she is losing her only opportunity*) But I didn't ask him. Everyone says you did, Father, but they don't know you the way I did. If you plead guilty to murder, it's what they call a technicality. That still wouldn't mean you did it. You'd just have a better chance.

RIVARD: What chance?

AMOS: Come on, Erna.

ERNA: (*Explaining what she has heard but does not fully understand or approve of*) If you say you're guilty, no matter what the jury thinks, they can only sentence you to life. They can't hang you.

RIVARD: Do you think I'm guilty, Erna? That I could kill Sister Rita?

ERNA: (*Uncertainly*) No.

(Toby Felker appears. He once had dreams of being an important lawyer, but his wife wanted to return to Solon after Toby graduated from the University of Michigan. She wanted to live and be buried in Solon. She did and was. Toby was left alone, without his dream, without a reason)

ERNA: He's here.

(Erna exits)

TOBY: *(Enters cell)* Toby Felker. *(Attempts to shake hands with handcuffed Rivard)* Oh, come on, Amos.

(Amos removes handcuffs)

Don't pay him any mind. Young men hereabouts don't amount to much, and I don't know why. I was burning up with ambition when I was their age. *(To Amos)* You can wait outside now.

AMOS: Have to protect you, Toby.

TOBY: You have to listen so you can tell that crowd out there what's happening. You go out right now or I'm telling the sheriff—

AMOS: *(To Rivard)* If you take him for your lawyer, you better be sure you're pleading guilty 'cause he ain't ever got nobody off, everybody knows it, too.

TOBY: *(Calling)* Sheriff.

AMOS: *(As he exits)* Toby. I was going to do a chore anyway.

TOBY: *(To Rivard)* You don't remember me, do you?

RIVARD: No.

TOBY: I met you once. A Grange meeting in Leland.

You were sharp as a pin at the Grange. Explaining why Catholics have Mass and everything. Don't you remember? I was the one who introduced you and conducted the question and answer period.

(Rivard clearly does not remember, which momentarily disappoints Toby)

Now I got to tell you, you don't have to take me as your lawyer. You don't. But if you don't, you should know, for one thing, I'm the only lawyer out here on the peninsula. Now there isn't much for a lawyer out here, you know. 'Cept after the spring rains move the creeks hither and thither. Arguing boundary disputes, if you know what I mean. But you don't have to take me. Maurice told me the smelt are running down at Boyne City, and I wouldn't mind getting a barrel of 'em. You fish?

RIVARD: No.

TOBY: You don't expect to see a priest fishing, come to think of it.

RIVARD: Do you want my case?

TOBY: Sure. Sure I want your case. Do you accept me? That's the point.

RIVARD: As long as you believe I'm innocent.

TOBY: Innocent?

RIVARD: Yes.

TOBY: But that means a trial. And I'd have to know, well, a lot. Yes. A lot. *(He sits. Takes from pocket old envelope on which to make notes)* What did happen that last day? The day of the fire. Four and a half years ago. You both disappeared the same night. Everyone figured . . . but you tell me, what did happen?

RIVARD: I don't know. I know nothing happened. It couldn't have. I'm not a violent man.

TOBY: All right. All right. We could start at the beginning. Why did you send for another nun?

(*Sister Rita appears behind Rivard*)

RIVARD: The other two sisters were ill.

TOBY: Did you ask for a young one?

RIVARD: There was so much she'd have to . . . I can't live through it again.

TOBY: Exactly when did she arrive?

RIVARD: About this time of year. There were lilacs. It seemed late. I mean, I had expected her about an hour earlier. I walked out to the road to see if I could see her coming up from the valley. No. That's all.

(*Sister Rita steps closer. She is very young for a nun, and pretty in her youth. She has not yet learned to hold back first, natural responses. She carries a bunch of lilacs and a rattan suitcase. She is warm, having walked up the steep hill on which Holy Rosary and its adjacent buildings sleep. Now at the top, she stops and looks back at the valley's toylike town. Rivard sees her. Toby does not. He freezes and is unaware of what happens when Rivard enters the past*)

SISTER RITA: I didn't think it would be beautiful. All those trees. It's almost a wilderness.

TOBY: How can I help you if—?

RIVARD: Some other time. We'll talk some other—

SISTER RITA: (*Overlapping Rivard*) I barely slept on the train for imagining what Solon would be like.

RIVARD: No. No. I don't want to remember.

SISTER RITA: Every house down there has lilacs, doesn't it? I picked these down there along the road. The Bishop told me the Indian name for Solon was "Land of Rainbows."

THE HILL

(Rivard crosses to Sister Rita with an abrupt change of attitude. He is open, vigorous, truly pleased to see Sister Rita)

PRIEST: *(Accepting lilacs)* Yes, they're fond of the Indian names at the chancery, but it has been a long time since there's been a rainbow at Solon. We're experiencing a drought. But they wouldn't know that.

SISTER RITA: That's why there are no birds. It's so peculiar, all those trees and not a single bird. You can almost smell the dryness.

PRIEST: According to Indian superstition the birds leave before a forest fire.

SISTER RITA: Oh, I hope not, Father. In Detroit, where I grew up, there were just scraggly trees along the street. Now this forest—

PRIEST: You'll weary of the trees, Sister.

SISTER RITA: Impossible, Father. I just fell in love.

PRIEST: An infatuation.

SISTER RITA: No infatuations before the convent. Certainly not after, Father.

PRIEST: But eventually the trees can bother you. The

winter is long up here, and the trees sometimes seem to be closing in on you. I find the best thing to do is to just keep busy. Then there's no time for homesickness or any melancholy over what you renounced. You won't want that in your mind up here. Not because of any rule, but just because it might slow you down.

SISTER RITA: They used to say that at Guardian Angel as if it would comfort me. But I don't believe it, Father. It was a new life when I entered the convent, yes. But I was alive before. I believe everything I've done is part of me. I had to be a child then to be a nun now. I've kept a diary. Since I was old enough to write really. When I look through it now, I see that most of the worries I had at fifteen I have today. The present is little more than a mirror of the past. *(Happy to share one of her deepest convictions)* I am a person who is a nun, not a nun who used to be a person.

PRIEST: *(Not wanting to disagree)* Well, Mrs. Shandig is my housekeeper. Neither Sister Immaculata nor Sister Mary Martha have been well lately, so Mrs. Shandig can help you to—

SISTER RITA: I shouldn't have spoken so plainly. I've angered you.

PRIEST: Not at all.

SISTER RITA: Would you wait then?

PRIEST: Why?

SISTER RITA: You're annoyed with me.

PRIEST: I'm not annoyed.

SISTER RITA: But you seem so—

PRIEST: What do you want?

SISTER RITA: The Church. There is a certain prayer—
I promised my saint it would be the first—

PRIEST: You certainly don't need to apologize for praying.

SISTER RITA: Father. Please don't be angry before you know me.

PRIEST: I am not angry. Except by the fact that you keep telling me that I am.

SISTER RITA: I'm sorry.

(Silence)

PRIEST: The other sisters, they never talk much. At least not with me, but then what could they. . . . But I do enjoy exchanging ideas, I do. But the people up here. They respect the Church, but they expect that priests. . . . You know. I think I'm out of practice.

SISTER RITA: I think conversation is as essential as air. If people don't talk with each other, what good is anything?

PRIEST: You know, when I first came to Solon I too made a completely terrible start.

SISTER RITA: I don't feel I've made a completely terrible start.

PRIEST: No. No, you haven't. I didn't mean that. But when I came to Solon, I was the first priest appointed to Holy Rosary in nine years. The bishop didn't even know if the church would still be here. But you know how eager Bishop Ginter is to expand, which is why I think he sent me here. And also I needed a quiet parish to work on my book. It's called "Augustinian Order (colon) An Examination and Extension." And surprisingly enough, what with starting the school, convincing the men to build the convent, converting one of them in the process, and . . . well, the book is coming along. Not as fast as I'd hoped because. . . . At any rate, when I arrived here, no one met me. I asked the blacksmith for directions. Maurice Prindle, the blacksmith, is rather a practical joker and he sent me to that little church down there. And when I saw the sign "Solon Evangelical Methodist," I thought—

THE CELL

TOBY: Rivard, listen to me.

RIVARD: (*Crossing to Toby*) I did not kill Sister Rita. There's very little to hold on to. I've doubted my sanity at moments. I believe in God, the Father Almighty. There's that. But I don't have the Church, all the helps that other — (*Interrupting himself, no longer able to conceal his deepest fear*) She haunted me.

TOBY: Rivard. Let's just say. Let's just say, I don't understand, Rivard.

RIVARD: She did. When I left here. For a long time it kept—

TOBY: Rivard. Get ahold of yourself.

RIVARD: It's true. She never left my side. No matter what I did. I needed some kind of order. In Detroit I worked on the assembly line. I worked very hard. There's endless overtime, you see, and I took it all just so I wouldn't think. I moved my hands back and forth and the shiny parts came and went on the two black belts. Just so I'd be tired and could sleep. But it failed. The harder I worked, the more I saw her.

TOBY: Sister Rita.

RIVARD: Yes. I'd go to the room at night and I would fall asleep, but then my hands would just start moving, working like in the factory, back and forth. From the assembly line, you know. And then I'd be awake. The room was black, empty, but there would be this lightness, a presence, her. I thought maybe it was the place. Maybe by some coincidence she had lived near that place when she was a girl. It had those scraggly trees which she had talked about. So I moved. I moved so many times. And then, now, the last few months it's . . . abated. And I'm afraid to have it back. I can't.

TOBY: Father, do you hear yourself? You talk like a guilty man.

RIVARD: You don't understand. You see, the only time I actually approached happiness was during these last few months in Detroit. No one knew my name. No one expected anything of me. I want to live like that again. Working. Walking. Eating. Sleeping. No past. No future. Just a very small present.

TOBY: That's the kind of thinking your theology gets you into, Father. See, I understand something about you Catholics. And I don't mind. I believe you are innocent. I don't know why. Just instinct, I guess. What you people call a leap of faith. But I've got to have hard facts, Father. Now, I don't suppose there's any I could get the jury to believe the nun committed suicide.

RIVARD: No.

TOBY: Now, she was dead when you left, right?

RIVARD: They told me in Detroit when they arrested me. I didn't know she died.

TOBY: She was alive when you left.

RIVARD: Yes.

TOBY: You're certain.

RIVARD: Yes.

TOBY: Then that's it.

RIVARD: What?

TOBY: Your defense. I got it. I have got it. It doesn't matter *why*, but *when* you left. And *who* saw you who can testify she was still alive. The other nuns? How in hell do you suppose you subpoena nuns? Remember that day, Father. Who? Who saw you leave that knows you left before Sister Rita was killed? That housekeeper of yours, ah, Mrs. Shandig?

RIVARD: I don't remember.

TOBY: Well, you had to come through town, right? Who saw you? Maurice? He's always sitting out front.

RIVARD: Yes. I talked to him. Maurice. I asked, I asked him to do a chore for me up at Holy Rosary.

TOBY: Good. (*Calling*) Amos.

RIVARD: Yes. I can remember. You'll help me. I am strong enough. I'll remember every detail, and then it will be over.

TOBY: (*Shaking Rivard's hand*) Now that I've got a handle on this, I know I can do good work. I'm good. Hell, I'm already better than I thought I'd be. (*Seeing Amos enter*) Good-bye for now.

(*Amos and Toby exit*)

(*Rivard hears children singing "The Lilac Song." He turns to listen and sees Mrs. Shandig enter. She is round and*

*could have been the epitome of the wholesome midwestern
mother if not widowed so early. She has a deep sense of
her lowly position, which she enjoys)*

BACK PORCH

*(Priest is in study, enjoying the opportunity to overhear
the pleasant exchange about to happen. The singing turns
into the sound of children laughing. Mrs. Shandig leaves
her kitchen to see what the laughing is all about. Sister
Rita enters and crosses, nearly running with school papers.
Mrs. Shandig startles Sister Rita when she speaks)*

MRS. SHANDIG: Sister. What's wrong?

SISTER RITA: Mrs. Shandig, don't tell Father. I forgot
their compositions so I ran back to the convent while—

MRS. SHANDIG: But the noise, Sister. And laughing.

SISTER RITA: Yes. It's Louise doing her celebrated im-
itation of me. She has no idea that I know. You could
have watched them for me. I never even thought of—

MRS. SHANDIG: Oh no. I never go to the school.

SISTER RITA: *(Showing her composition)* This is
Louise's. Look at that. She writes so well.

MRS. SHANDIG: Oh yes. It's very neat.

SISTER RITA: Just read a little of it. I have to get back.
You'll see how well she—

MRS. SHANDIG: *(Starting toward kitchen)* No. I don't
have time.

SISTER RITA: *(Stopping her)* Mrs. Shandig?

MRS. SHANDIG: Yes.

SISTER RITA: Oh, just . . . remember, if you ever want to sit in the back of class to listen, to the singing or whatever—

MRS. SHANDIG: Sister. Sister, ever since you came, I wanted to ask you . . .

SISTER RITA: What?

MRS. SHANDIG: Father doesn't have to teach since you're here, but he works even harder on his book since you came. I worry about him.

SISTER RITA: Why?

MRS. SHANDIG: He's in that study from Mass 'til supper most days. And I thought if I could read some of the books for him, I could tell him what's in them and then he wouldn't get so tired and irritable. I want to help him, but I don't . . . Well, you see . . .

SISTER RITA: I could teach you to read, Mrs. Shandig.

MRS. SHANDIG: Do you think I can learn reading?

SISTER RITA: Of course.

MRS. SHANDIG: I am older, you know.

SISTER RITA: Anyone who knows the entire Mass by heart . . . I saw your lips following the Mass.

MRS. SHANDIG: I wasn't always. . . . I'm only a convert, Sister. Father Rivard, he brought me into the Church. *(Suddenly remembering her responsibility)* Oh. I'm doing my bread.

(Mrs. Shandig crosses to kitchen table and begins to knead the dough)

THE KITCHEN

(Sister Rita hesitates, then follows Mrs. Shandig)

SISTER RITA: When did all that happen?

MRS. SHANDIG: Two and a half years ago. When I came to Solon. I was married before. *(Exhilarated by the opportunity for a long hoped-for conversation, Mrs. Shandig is becoming somewhat flustered)* Oh, no, I forgot about his eggnog.

SISTER RITA: Here, I'll do that for you.

(Sister Rita sits in chair to make eggnog)

MRS. SHANDIG: *(Continuing kneading)* Thank you, Sister. I never knew very much. Cooking and cleaning, just that. I always worked at a camp. Lumbering. Those men. You wouldn't know how they are, Sister. If I tell you, you wouldn't like me.

SISTER RITA: You know that isn't true.

MRS. SHANDIG: But the students are waiting for you.

SISTER RITA: I left Louise in charge. Right now you're more important, Mrs. Shandig.

MRS. SHANDIG: I am? Well, my husband, he did the hunting for them at the camp. He brought me those bleeding animals. As long as I can remember I had to skin them and cook their bloody meat. Every day I hoped he wouldn't come back. I did. Sister, I even prayed he wouldn't come back. Finally, then, he didn't come back. I thought it was my fault, but Father says it wasn't. I had to run away then. From those other men in the camp. Without him there, they changed to me. They started grabbing after me. Poking at me with their spoons. I can't tell you what happened. I told Father. *(Realizing she is becoming more intimate than she should)* I never saw a town until I saw Solon. I didn't. They told me down there that Father needed a housekeeper. I never knew there was Catholics before that. I didn't. Just God. I owe everything to Father, so I have to help as much as can be. I try to be the best Catholic I can for him, but it's harder. Me being only a convert.

SISTER RITA: They always told me that converts make the best Catholics. Did you know that? You can be proud of it. You made a choice. I never had a choice.

MRS. SHANDIG: Don't tell anyone I wasn't born Catholic. No one else knows. The other sisters even. But I try real hard to be good.

SISTER RITA: Sometime you look through Father's Saints Book and count how many of the saints were converts. You'll see.

MRS. SHANDIG: I can't read yet. I just want to.

SISTER RITA: *(Handing her a book)* Well, soon, Mrs. Shandig. Very soon.

(Sister Rita exits, followed by Mrs. Shandig. Toby enters and sits with Rivard. Prosecutor and Monsignor enter and go to witness stand)

THE COURTROOM

PROSECUTOR: At the time of the murder of Sister Rita, you were chief administrator of the Michigan diocese of the Holy Roman Church.

MONSIGNOR: I was and am Bishop Ginter's secretary. A position of greater responsibility than the title suggests.

PROSECUTOR: Did you visit the defendant in his cell this morning?

MONSIGNOR: I did.

PROSECUTOR: What was the purpose of your meeting this morning?

MONSIGNOR: I offered to hear confession.

PROSECUTOR: Did he accept the sacrament?

TOBY: (*Rising, crossing toward Prosecutor*) Objection. The prosecution is attempting to seek—what do you call it?

PROSECUTOR: Privileged communication.

TOBY: Privileged communication between the clergyman and the, ah, penitent.

PROSECUTOR: I wouldn't seek privileged communication. (*To Monsignor*) I repeat, did the defendant confess?

MONSIGNOR: No. He is no longer a practicing Catholic.

PROSECUTOR: Most reverend monsignor, how can it be that a priest of the Holy Roman Church could no longer be a practicing—

TOBY: I object to any derogatory reference to the defendant's religion. Which, incidentally, was not the Holy Roman Church, but simple, everyday Catholicism. If this were to be a religious inquisition, it would be held in other chambers.

(Prosecutor and Monsignor now freeze in position as light goes to half on them)

THE CELL

TOBY: I talked to Maurice about the last night. He did do the chore for you up at the church, but he didn't see Sister Rita.

RIVARD: But he must have.

TOBY: He'll swear under oath he didn't. *(Standing)* I'm asking the sherifff to see if he can locate your Mrs. Shandig, so don't be discouraged. I'll think of something.

(Toby exits. Mrs. Shandig enters with eggnog)

THE STUDY

MRS. SHANDIG: Father. Are you all right? *(Placing eggnog on desk, waiting for recognition)* Father, if I'm disturbing you, tell me, and I'll just—

PRIEST: *(Continuing desk work)* No. I'm glad you're here. I am.

MRS. SHANDIG: *(Pushing eggnog across desk)* Here. It's time for your eggnog.

PRIEST: You're determined to fatten me up, aren't you?

MRS. SHANDIG: Oh, Father, go on with you. *(Indicating he should drink, then crossing to open a window)* We all have to keep up our health with the other nuns so sickly. Can I ask you something, Father?

PRIEST: *(Indicating for her to sit)* Of course you can.

MRS. SHANDIG: It's personal, and I don't want to be prying, Father. I don't. Too thick don't mix, I always say.

PRIEST: *(Sitting, on edge of desk)* Now come on, Mrs. Shandig. *(Again indicating where she may sit)*

MRS. SHANDIG: *(Sitting, then after a moment)* You've seemed so bothered.

PRIEST: Of course I'm bothered. I have a great many things to worry about. *(Rising, pacing)* What do they expect of me? The Bishop wants me to write this book, which anyone knows is a nearly impossible task. Then they expect me to turn the buttons from the collection plate into food for five mouths, to baptize a county full of Protestants, and to get my six very poor farmers to find the time to build a second outhouse so that the boys and girls can have recess at the same time. And now on top of it all you expect me to drink the richest, most repulsive concoction since—

MRS. SHANDIG: *(Rising, taking glass from his hand)* You don't have to drink it. I'm only trying to help.

(She starts to exit)

PRIEST: I realize that. I'm sorry.

(He holds out hand for drink)

MRS. SHANDIG: Only if you want it.

PRIEST: I do.

(She hands it to him with pleasure. Priest drinks it in one swallow)

MRS. SHANDIG: Well, I guess it's best you say those things to me. Just so you don't have to talk out loud to yourself in the study.

PRIEST: You can hear me?

MRS. SHANDIG: Just a bit. Sometimes. I never understand about your writing problems, but if you talked with someone. . . .

PRIEST: (Crossing to window) Maybe if I could talk it out. . . . Then maybe it would clarify. You know who I could discuss my book with?

MRS. SHANDIG: (Following to window) Sister.

PRIEST: (Laughing) Yes. She's worked out well, hasn't she? School was over half an hour ago, and there's still a batch of them over there talking to her. It might be nice if I invited her over for supper some night.

MRS. SHANDIG: You'd be alone with a nun, Father.

PRIEST: Well, believe it or not, Mrs. Shandig, I am capable of remarkable propriety.

MRS. SHANDIG: Father, this once I know what's best. I don't think much else matters but what people think of you. Someone might see her leaving your house at night. What people see happening matters more than what you'd say afterwards. Everyone trusts their eyes. Hardly anyone trusts their ears. Father, everyone thinks you are the finest person that ever they knew.

PRIEST: And well they should, shouldn't they?

MRS. SHANDIG: I think so.

PRIEST: I care about other people, don't I?

22

MRS. SHANDIG: Yes, you do, Father.

PRIEST: Like Sister. With the other nuns ill. Sister has no one to eat with, and therefore—

MRS. SHANDIG: Father, you know nuns expect to be lonely.

PRIEST: No. No one expects that.

MRS. SHANDIG: Father, I don't like to see you like this. You should be happy here. What do I do wrong? I follow all the rules.

PRIEST: And they make us lonely. Why should the Church cause it? That's what I don't understand. Why do we cause it? Loneliness is not contagious, you know, yet people stand by and willingly watch others suffer as if they were afraid they'll catch it by intervening. It makes me wonder if we are naturally cruel. Something, here, inside, makes us, unlike God, revel in misery.

MRS. SHANDIG: Those are beautiful words, Father. Are they from your book?

PRIEST: Yes. They shouldn't be. You are certainly right this time, Mrs. Shandig. But I can't figure out how I can be so wrong all the—

(Sister Rita enters)

SISTER RITA: I hope I'm not interrupting. The children and I just had a wonderful idea. *(Silence)* What is wrong?

PRIEST: Shouldn't you have sent a note, Sister?

SISTER RITA: We just thought of it.

PRIEST: The other nuns always ask to see me first.

MRS. SHANDIG: Sister, it's only for the students. They'll be thinking it is right to come running over here whenever they want.

SISTER RITA: Father. I'm sorry.

PRIEST: Actually, I don't mind. I'm like you and tend to be too pragmatic, forgetting there may be excellent reasons for traditions that are momentarily troublesome, as Mrs. Shandig was just reminding me. Now, what have you and the students thought up?

SISTER RITA: Painting.

MRS. SHANDIG: What would they paint, Sister?

PRIEST: The cloakroom is covered with little handprints. A darker—

SISTER RITA: No. Pictures. Flowers, trees. Their houses.

PRIEST: That's good, Sister. I like it.

SISTER RITA: Thank you, Father.

PRIEST: The lives of the saints would make good subjects, and at Christmas they could—

SISTER RITA: We can even add it to the curriculum.

PRIEST: We don't have to do that. I'd have to ask the Bishop.

SISTER RITA: Tell him our problem. I've never seen children with so little sense of what is good in life. So little imagination.

PRIEST: Yes. I like the idea. Now we'll need paper.

SISTER RITA: There's plenty of composition paper, Father.

PRIEST: Now *your* imagination is wanting. Their world's got to be bigger than composition paper. Would it matter if the paper were tan?

SISTER RITA: Why?

PRIEST: There's a butcher in Traverse City who's Catholic.

MRS. SHANDIG: Bernard Christiansen.

PRIEST: When I take the other nuns into the doctor, I'll pay that butcher a visit.

MRS. SHANDIG: What about paints?

SISTER RITA: Maybe when you write the Bishop, he could send—

PRIEST: But I'd rather not write the Bishop.

MRS. SHANDIG: I have the Sears and Roebuck catalog in my room.

PRIEST: Good. We'll try that.

SISTER RITA: I could write the Bishop. He's very proud of me because—

PRIEST: No. I don't want you to. You might end up in as much difficulty as I am.

MRS. SHANDIG: What difficulty?

SISTER RITA: What do you mean?

PRIEST: Well, nothing really important, I suppose.

SISTER RITA: Well, I wouldn't care what they did to
me, Father. I wouldn't feel right having the children
paint during school time unless it was part of the curriculum. You know, Father, the very ones who most need
such an experience wouldn't stay after. That's for certain.

MRS. SHANDIG: What difficulty are you talking
about?

(Sister Rita and Mrs. Shandig remain frozen in place)

THE COURTROOM

PROSECUTOR: I understand that there had been no
priest assigned to Solon for nearly a decade prior to Father Rivard.

MONSIGNOR: Nine years.

PROSECUTOR: Why was such a change made?

MONSIGNOR: Father   Rivard's   particular   talents
seemed more useful up here.

PROSECUTOR: Was he sent to this out-of-the-way
post because he was a troublemaker?

MONSIGNOR: Father Rivard was incredibly energetic
and popular with parishioners and therefore a bit of an
aggravation to the senior priests wherever we put him.
The Bishop thought by bringing him into the chancery
he might personally be able to guide the young priest.
But Father Rivard did not readily accede to such help.
The Bishop had to request me to stop Father Rivard
from entering his office without an appointment. He
would burst in and no matter who was present bring up
an obscure theological point, suggest his ideas for raising

funds through games of chance as is done in certain eastern cities . . . And there was ultimately an incident of his usurping a responsibility that was distinctly the privilege of Bishop Ginter.

THE CHANCERY

(*A Gregorian chant can be heard distantly as Rivard walks to witness stand and then, as the young Priest, walks back across stage with Monsignor*)

PRIEST: You told me to look in on Mother Vincent.

MONSIGNOR: But not to give Last Rites. You knew the Bishop would visit in the morning.

PRIEST: She asked me to. She told me to. She was so feverish that she was nearly mad.

MONSIGNOR: She asked, did she?

PRIEST: Yes.

MONSIGNOR: Of course, you assume there would be no way for me to confirm that.

PRIEST: We were alone.

MONSIGNOR: Mother Vincent did not die.

PRIEST: Oh, I'm so glad. No one told me. Will she be—

MONSIGNOR: And she remembers nothing of requesting Last Rites. In fact—

PRIEST: Well, she was delirious and—

MONSIGNOR: Enough. You are to be assigned immediately to a parish far from the Bishopric.

PRIEST: You would punish me for being compassionate.

MONSIGNOR: Is that the way you see it?

PRIEST: I know Bishop Cinter would not—

MONSIGNOR: Father Rivard, I hardly think I need remind you again that I speak for the Bishop.

PRIEST: When a priest is asked to give the sacrament, he is bound to give it; she begged me. Did you want me to get a medical opinion? By that time she could have been dead.

MONSIGNOR: The Bishop assumes you've read St. Augustine. *Confessiones? De Civitate Dei?*

PRIEST: Of course.

MONSIGNOR: Have you read *De Fide Vero?*

PRIEST: *Of True Religion.*

MONSIGNOR: I didn't think a translation necessary. When still a young man, about your age I would say, Aurelius Augustinius, long before he was Bishop of Hippo, before he even thought of being consecrated Bishop . . . he went into a five-year period of seclusion while he wrote many philosophical studies. It tuned his mind, disciplined his spirit, and prepared him for the robes you are so eager to don. And so shall you. Read *Of True Religion* closely, carefully. Then write your concept of the Church's authority. When your study is completed, in a couple of years I would say, I shall read it. When I have read it, the Bishop will read it. And we shall discuss your new understanding and your future.

PRIEST: I won't do it.

MONSIGNOR: Why?

PRIEST: Priests are assigned according to the needs of the parish and the talents of—

MONSIGNOR: Enough. Questioning dogma. Then usurping the Bishop's responsibility. Now scattering Last Rites to the living like a housewife feeding fowl. Enough. Quite enough. I have located a parish that will suit your contemplative pursuits.

PRIEST: I am not a contemplative man. I want to serve where I can do the most good. You don't know me if you'd waste the good I'm capable of.

MONSIGNOR: Of which you are capable. The Indian name for Solon was "Land of Rainbows." Attractive, peaceful. Perfect for the seclusion St. Augustine similarly sought in his preparation for becoming a bishop.

PRIEST: I won't go until I speak to the Bishop.

MONSIGNOR: He is consecrating a church in Saginaw. He left you a letter. He wishes you God's speed.

(Monsignor makes sign of cross and exits)

THE STUDY

SISTER RITA: One reason. Just one reason I can understand why you won't write the Bishop for permission for painting. That's all I ask.

PRIEST: *(Crossing to Sister Rita)* Well, maybe I've gotten a bit gun-shy, Sister. What do you think?

SISTER RITA: We will all say a prayer that the Bishop will fill your request, Father. (*Leaving*) Remember, through page seventeen Saturday, Mrs. Shandig.

MRS. SHANDIG: Yes, Sister. I already read it twice.

SISTER RITA: That's good. Then see if you can go as far as twenty-one. Thank you, Father. (*As she exits*) Children. Father said yes. He'll hear from the Bishop in just a few. . . .

THE CELL

TOBY: (*Crossing from courtroom*) What about this business I've heard tell that Sister Rita lived with you?

RIVARD: She didn't live with me. It was an emergency measure. That's all. She stayed in the rectory. We seldom even ate together.

TOBY: Then why didn't you tell me before? I've got two days. These circuit judges don't smile on long trials, Father. Don't withhold information from me.

RIVARD: It's not important.

TOBY: That prosecutor can build his whole case on this. High enough to hang a noose. He's good. He's young. At the rate he's going, why with cases like this, he'll be writing laws in Lansing before he's thirty-five. With a motive like that, the jury won't hesitate to hang you. Crime of passion. This is exactly the kind of thing Protestants are sure happens behind those heavy lace curtains in rectories. If there is one thing they hate more than Catholics out here, it's sex. People hate what they don't understand. Why did you take her out of the convent and into the house with you?

RIVARD: I had to let her live there. I had to.

TOBY: Why?

RIVARD: The other sisters had consumption. They could not be moved.

TOBY: *(Standing right of Rivard)* Couldn't you send Sister Rita to another convent?

(Sister Rita enters and remains left of Rivard)

RIVARD: I was afraid we'd have to close the school.

SISTER RITA: Father, I can't believe you'd even think of closing the school.

TOBY: Why would you have to close the school? I don't understand.

RIVARD: I couldn't teach all the classes.

SISTER RITA: Mrs. Shandig said I have to leave because—

TOBY: But you taught before the nuns came.

SISTER RITA: Not all by yourself. We could share the teaching and keep the school open.

TOBY: Why did she have to live in the rectory of all places? Come on, Rivard. You said you're strong enough. For God's sake, give me some help.

(Rivard turns away from Toby)

RIVARD: The doctor said she couldn't live under the same roof with two consumptives.

(Toby exits)

SISTER RITA: There are rooms to rent above Maurice's blacksmith shop.

THE CLASSROOM

PRIEST: It would be too dangerous. Last year they broke into Widow Webber's house and—

SISTER RITA: Then up here. The rectory. Your house.

PRIEST: Your community wouldn't allow it. Sister, we have Holy Laws to guide us.

SISTER RITA: I believe the Church stands for people, not laws. If you wrote Mother Vincent, she'd realize—

PRIEST: (Sitting on edge of table) I wish I could. Priests don't deal with the Mother House. Only the Bishop.

SISTER RITA: Ask him for a dispensation. Then Mother Vincent would have to—

PRIEST: Sister, this is not easy, but it must be. It must be.

SISTER RITA: Very little must be, Father. Please. God knows everything we do is for the Church. He knows we do it for the sake of His children. (Showing Priest students' drawings) They are responding, learning from me. They need me, Father. It could be months before there'd be another teaching assignment for me again. (Calming down as Priest shows interest in drawings) I don't think they believe I'm a very good teacher. They didn't really want to send me up here, but I have been good. Haven't I?

PRIEST: (Standing) This is not a personal question. I built the school. I want it open.

SISTER RITA: But this is my responsibility.

PRIEST: Your spiritual guidance, your life in Christ, is my responsibility.

SISTER RITA: And what about your responsibility to the children?

PRIEST: You want to break the laws for yourself, not the children. You feel useful. That's the sin of pride.

SISTER RITA: And you? Keeping the school open all by yourself. How good would that be for the children?

PRIEST: I am trying to do the best I can, Sister. I cannot do more.

SISTER RITA: What have I done wrong? Why do you want me to leave?

PRIEST: I didn't say I want you to leave. This is not a personal question. Why do you always insist upon making everything a personal question?

THE STUDY

MRS. SHANDIG: The letter's here. From the Bishop, Father. He won't let Sister move in here.

(Rivard crosses to desk, sits, opens letter)

I'm certain of it. I don't know why you even asked him.

PRIEST: *(Reading letter)* Mrs. Shandig, he gave permission for you to live here.

MRS. SHANDIG: But I'm not a nun. I'm not. That makes all the difference.

(Priest finishes reading. Silence. Mrs. Shandig sits)

What did he tell you, Father?

PRIEST: He doesn't want me to close the school.

MRS. SHANDIG: But Sister. What does he say about Sister?

PRIEST: Nothing. He didn't mention her.

MRS. SHANDIG: No. He had to. He told you she can't live here, didn't he?

PRIEST: "I am stunned to read that you considered suspending classes at the very time our diocese is enjoying the most rapid rate of expansion of any in America. Your fine record cannot but reassure me that you have already resolved your local administrative problem without further need of advice from me. I am certain you are finding staying in the village uncomfortable, but it will surely not be for long." The Bishop didn't answer me. It's Monsignor, that hypocrite.

(Priest rips letter, throws pieces on floor)

MRS. SHANDIG: *(Kneeling to pick up letter)* Father, what's wrong? You mustn't talk so.

PRIEST: *(Kneeling to talk with her)* You hear what he wants. He wants me to live in town. To leave four women defenseless on this hill.

MRS. SHANDIG: No. You can't live down there. Those men are vicious. They're vicious, Father. I go down every day. I know.

SISTER RITA: *(From classroom)* Do you want me to leave?

PRIEST: Do you want Sister to live down there?

MRS. SHANDIG: No, Father.

SISTER RITA: Everything we do is for the Church.

(Sister Rita exits)

PRIEST: *(Rises)* Here then. My house. I'll go and tell her.

MRS. SHANDIG: Father, no. *(Standing)* The Church has a rule so we—

PRIEST: I know Church law only too well, certainly better than you, and I don't require your services to remind me.

MRS. SHANDIG: Oh, Father. Father. Why do you talk like this? I only want to help. It's wrong for Sister to move in here. I just know it.

PRIEST: I believe it is the Will of God that we keep the school open. I'm sorry if your interpretation is different from mine.

MRS. SHANDIG: *(Suddenly crying)* Oh, Father. Please. I'm trying. I don't know what to do for you anymore. I just want to be so good for you.

PRIEST: No more now. No crying. Everything will be all right.

GUARD'S VOICE: The Prosecution calls Miss Louise Donnelly for the People.

(Louise, Prosecutor, and Toby enter. Mrs. Shandig exits)

THE COURTROOM

(Louise, a college girl with all the liberation and pretension of half an education, is on the stand. Rivard sits with Toby)

LOUISE: Yes. As a matter of fact, it was she who first suggested I had the potentiality for college. No girl from Solon would ever have thought of such a thing. I have just completed one semester at Central Normal. I am, in a sense, indebted to Sister Rita. She had flaws, I suppose, being a nun and all.

PROSECUTOR: Did you know Father Rivard?

LOUISE: Yes.

PROSECUTOR: How would you describe him?

LOUISE: We liked him. That is, until Sister moved into the rectory.

PROSECUTOR: She moved into the priest's house.

LOUISE: I remember the day. It was like a holiday. All Sister did was lead games and teach songs. That night she moved into his house. By the next morning everyone knew she was living in the rectory with him.

THE DINING ROOM

(Mrs. Shandig is setting table as Sister Rita enters with flowers)

SISTER RITA: Rather a sad offering I'm afraid. But this is my first evening, my first dinner. . . . I wanted to bring you something. Are there any flowers up here in the summer? I saw you planting your garden, Mrs. Shandig, but you only planted vegetables.

(Mrs. Shandig is about to comment negatively)

PRIEST: You're right. That's what's missing up here. Flowers. I suppose I could transplant some lilacs up from the valley. But they wouldn't have much of a chance if I did. I don't have the knack for making things grow. They are usually green for the exact length of time they take to die.

SISTER RITA: Listen, if you'll get the lilacs, I could start a garden down the hill a bit, and then they'll see the flowers when they look up at Holy Rosary. I haven't had a garden since I was fourteen, when they took me to Guardian Angel.

(*Mrs. Shandig exits. Silence*)

PRIEST: (*Awkwardly*) How are Sister Martha and Sister Immaculata tonight?

SISTER RITA: They feel well enough to envy me moving here. Especially Sister Martha. She's the clever one, you know. She was joking.

(*Silence*)

PRIEST: It will be cool after dinner, so I thought we might have dessert in my study. I laid the fire with birch.

SISTER RITA: That's very thoughtful, Father. Thank you.

PRIEST: Sometimes it's good to plan ahead, to look forward a bit.

(*He awkwardly indicates she may sit, pushes chair in too hard, sits down himself. Silence*)

SISTER RITA: Planning ahead can be the best part sometimes, though, don't you think, Father? (*Silence*) I saw Governor Pingree once. We planned it for two months. A group of novices went on the train to Lansing. The Fourth of July. I keep a diary and I wrote down everything. The stops the train made. How many books are in the library. The number of steps at the Capitol. The Governor's—

PRIEST: Everything.

SISTER RITA: Oh yes, everything. When my aunt came to visit me later, she looked at my postal cards. And for once I could tell my aunt things . . .

PRIEST: Didn't your aunt like to talk with you?

SISTER RITA: Well, I think communicating is very important. For me conversation is as essential as breathing.

PRIEST: I've noticed.

SISTER RITA: But my aunt. I loved her, Father, but I wasn't her niece. Not really. She was paid to keep . . . take care of me. Her husband had an accident in the barn with the horse. He was in bed without ever waking up for several days before he died. My aunt, she blamed me. She said the accident was my fault. I was playing up in the loft and . . . in a way it was. I had to sit by his bed then. I was so scared. I didn't know what was to become of me if he died. I watched a sparrow in the garden, and he made me laugh. My aunt heard me laughing. It made her so mad that she said terrible, cruel—that nobody loved me or would ever love me. She said no one would ever even talk with me after what I'd— (Stopping to fight back her tears) I don't know exactly what happened. There were days when . . . well, they said the priest, Father Walling, could hear me when he came and made her unlock me. He took me away, to Guardian Angel Convent, and the good sisters watched over me. (Crying somewhat, then controlling herself) That's what you meant. The first day. Not thinking of the past.

(Silence)

PRIEST: Maybe Mrs. Shandig has forgotten we're here. (Standing and calling to kitchen) Mrs. Shandig, we're ready to eat. (To Sister Rita as he paces) It's a stew. I always sample what she's cooking in the afternoon. It's good.

SISTER RITA: Since Mrs. Shandig has Thursdays for her day off, I thought you might like it if I cooked for us.

PRIEST: That would be splendid. But only if you'll have the time.

(Mrs. Shandig has entered)

SISTER RITA: I'll have time. If I'm going to live here, I want to do my share. And that should make it a bit easier on you, Mrs. Shandig. *(Silence)* Is there a little jug, Mrs. Shandig? We could put some water in it, and the flowers might be pretty on the—

MRS. SHANDIG: We don't have anything the right size, Sister.

SISTER RITA: Even a glass would be—

(Mrs. Shandig moves to exit)

PRIEST: Mrs. Shandig. Please bring me a glass for them. I haven't seen flowers where I lived since I was a young man. I'd like it. Put them in my study, and you can put one of your doilies under it.

MRS. SHANDIG: Yes, Father.

(Mrs. Shandig exits)

SISTER RITA: I think I must have hurt Mrs. Shandig somehow. Maybe in her reading lesson.

PRIEST: She likes flowers, I think.

SISTER RITA: Well, have I offended her? I'd apologize.

(Priest cuts off conversation by bowing his head and crossing himself)

SISTER RITA and PRIEST: *(Praying)* Bless us, oh Lord, and these Thy gifts which we are about to receive from Thy bounty through Christ our Lord. Amen.

PRIEST: No. It was me. I offended her. Mrs. Shandig thinks I should not eat with you. She thinks there would be . . . ramifications.

SISTER RITA: But there are none. Mrs. Shandig is in the house. I knew she would be, so it is entirely permissible for me to eat with you. This is exactly what Sister Martha was teasing me about.

PRIEST: People always want to think the worst. I remember when I was a young man, in my teens actually, I fell terribly and instantly in love with a merchant's daughter who wore blonde sausage curls. It's quite true. No nice girl in our town had ever dared to wear sausage curls, but this girl was from a good family and she did. It all would have come to naught except she found my eyelashes to be a "marvel of the modern world." Those were her words I'm afraid. Every now and again I see my eyelashes in a looking glass, and still I don't understand her fascination. But it was real enough for her, and we were inseparable, even thinking it would be romantic if we could convince the priest to let us make confession together. Everyone expected the worst would happen to us. My uncle, two cousins, our priest and the barber, all told me in increasing detail what a girl with sausage curls would expect of me, and how it would ruin my life. They would not relent. They fussed and tore at me like dogs with a knotted sock. Things I never knew the name of before then became everyday threats, hourly horrors finally. I couldn't think of anything but what they expected. Then she was sent away. Humiliated in front of everyone, and it was my. . . . There. I'm talking of my past.

(He stands)

SISTER RITA: Don't be unrealistic in what you expect of yourself, Father. Everyone thinks of the past. It's natural.

PRIEST: I think it's the Baptists, they stand up and tell what sins they committed before being saved. I've always thought that if I did that, if people knew what I was, how I thought before I entered the priesthood, people would either reject me outright or they would know how essential the Church is for a decent life. The Church is the most beautiful institution of which I can conceive. A wonder, like the greatest work of art. Perfectly logical and divine. Making absolute order from absolute chaos. The Church makes my life, any life, possible. Yet during the past winter here with these slow country people, the sisters both sick, it seemed as though—well, I weakened. I wondered if the Church were as perfect as I believed. Then you came, with your vitality, your joy in the Church, and all my enthusiasm returned. But now, people talking about you moving in here . . .

(Priest takes her hand)

It's like a cloud settling on us. Sometimes, sometimes I nearly despair there will ever be justice in people.

SISTER RITA: *(Putting other hand on Priest's which holds hers)* We don't always see it, I know, but God is just. And we couldn't know God if justice weren't in us.

(Priest withdraws hand as he realizes what has happened)

PRIEST: This, Sister, this now, is exactly why people think nuns and priests should not be alone together.

SISTER RITA: I don't know—

PRIEST: This kind of informal conversation encourages what I feared would—encourages a lack of discipline. *(Pause)* We, we won't be able to take our meals together.

SISTER RITA: But Father, when we talk, everything seems all right.

PRIEST: What does that mean?

SISTER RITA: Like I'm a person. I am so weary of hearing Sister's rosary, Sister's book, Sister's this, Sister's that. Never just hers.

PRIEST: It is not for us to worry how we are feeling. We must be separate from the world. All that chaos.

SISTER RITA: God isn't separate. Not from the world. Not from the things people do and feel. He came to earth as a baby. He worked as a carpenter, drank wine, loved the children. We are like God. You can't make God into something else than what you already know. If you do, then you're making God into your image. And God made us in—

PRIEST: (Angry) Sister. (Smiling) Oh, Sister, do you know, you sound very much like a Protestant?

THE COURTROOM

PROSECUTOR: Were there any other unusual changes after Sister started living with the priest?

LOUISE: Sophie . . . she was another student . . . Sophie and I, we had a great fiction between us that the priest and Sister were in love. We even talked—

PROSECUTOR: Did I hear right? "In love"?

TOBY: (Standing) Objection. The testimony reads: "Sophie and I had a great fiction. . . ."

PROSECUTOR: What gave rise to this fiction?

LOUISE: Well, for example . . . when he went into town, Sister would watch him through the window riding down, while she taught. He was, still is, a very attractive man.

TOBY: Mr. Rivard's appeal to the witness has never been in question.

PROSECUTOR: Did you ever confront either the sister or the priest with your opinions, Louise?

LOUISE: Yes. Sophie dared me to ask Sister Rita why priests and nuns couldn't marry.

THE STUDY

PRIEST: (*To Louise, still on witness stand*) Sister tells me you are full of questions these days, Louise.

LOUISE: So is Sophie.

PRIEST: I didn't ask to see you so I could punish you.

(*Louise follows Priest to desk*)

LOUISE: Then why?

PRIEST: To see if I can't answer some of your questions. (*Silence*) I thought it might be nice for us to have a conversation.

LOUISE: Your house is nice, Father.

PRIEST: Thank you.

(*Silence*)

LOUISE: Sister Rita's nice.

PRIEST: A good teacher.

LOUISE: Better than Sister Immaculata. She's crabby.

PRIEST: She's not well you know.

LOUISE: Do you think Sister Rita is nice, Father?

PRIEST: Yes.

LOUISE: How much?

PRIEST: What do you mean?

LOUISE: I like her a lot.

PRIEST: You should.

LOUISE: Do you?

PRIEST: How much do you think about this?

LOUISE: What?

PRIEST: Sister and I.

LOUISE: Never.

PRIEST: Lies are venial sins, Louise.

LOUISE: I thought you liked me.

PRIEST: That's why I want to help you.

LOUISE: You don't like me.

PRIEST: Louise. I like you. All right?

LOUISE: If you did you'd tell me things.

PRIEST: What things?

LOUISE: Things.

PRIEST: It is very hard to carry on a conversation with you, Louise.

LOUISE: What if someone loved you?

PRIEST: I see.

LOUISE: Priests love everyone, don't they?

PRIEST: Yes. Everyone. And that's not love to marry by. Love between a man and a woman isn't controlled by ideals as it is when you, say, you love people, everyone. Understand?

LOUISE: No.

PRIEST: Love between a man and a woman is unordered.

LOUISE: Families are ordered.

PRIEST: Married love is totally consuming. It takes time, frustration, and a great deal of effort. Specific people have specific needs. Not general needs as when you love everyone. See, you care so much that all you want to do is meet the other person's needs, make her happy. No matter what it may be. But you see, if she loves you, she doesn't care about her own needs. She only cares about yours. So she can't possibly tell you what she needs because she only needs to please you. Yet you have to find something you can do. Then, all the time, you worry if you are doing the right thing. Now that I think of it, I wonder that anyone goes to the trouble.

LOUISE: Oh, I know why.

PRIEST: I doubt you do.

LOUISE: I understand things so well when you explain them. I love your devotions.

PRIEST: Thank you.

LOUISE: So tell me, Father.

PRIEST: What?

(Mrs. Shandig enters with two eggnogs)

LOUISE: What would you do if someone said they loved you?

PRIEST: Sister Rita and I have to be clear-headed to help people, Louise. How could we be married, worried about each other, bothered about ice bills and the children's teeth?

LOUISE: I didn't mean Sister Rita. Just anyone. Anyone at all. What would you say?

(Silence)

PRIEST: There are things, young lady, that are a sin even to think about, let alone say. One has to discipline one's mind as well as actions. And you remember that. To think something is as great a sin as to do it.

LOUISE: *(To Mrs. Shandig as she takes the glass)* Thank you. There aren't raw eggs in this, are there?

MRS. SHANDIG: It's good for you.

LOUISE: *(Aftering taking a sip)* Ich. I hate raw eggs. Can I go?

PRIEST: Of course.

LOUISE: Bye.

(Louise exits to witness stand)

MRS. SHANDIG: *(As she exits with glasses)* Those are some ideas she has there, Father.

PRIEST: Yes, aren't they.

THE COURTROOM

PROSECUTOR: Do you think you could have imagined there was a romance because being such an obviously aware, intelligent child, you did observe precisely the telling details which could lead to the only possible logical conclusion?

LOUISE: The priest was having carnal knowledge of the nun.

TOBY: *(Laughing)* That's not the only conclusion. It's certainly not a possible conclusion. And it is not a logical conclusion. I don't even think it is a conclusion.

PROSECUTOR: I withdraw the question. Your witness.

TOBY: Now, Louise. Did you ever imagine the priest in bed?

LOUISE: I don't know. Probably I did.

TOBY: Who was in bed with the priest in your fantasies? Who did you imagine?

LOUISE: I guess Sister Rita.

TOBY: Now, Louise, what do you guess you imagined them doing?

LOUISE: I didn't know then about . . . such things.

TOBY: You didn't.

LOUISE: Just, well, sounds. I imagined sounds. That's all.

TOBY: Did you ever imagine someone other than Sister Rita. Up there. In bed. With the priest. Making sounds? Anyone at all? *(Silence)* Did you confess your fantasies to the priest?

LOUISE: He was most cruel and extreme in his penance.

TOBY: Extreme?

LOUISE: Especially after the Monsignor visited.

TOBY: He was even stricter after the Monsignor visited?

LOUISE: He forbade me having lunch with the other children and instead made me say endless Hail Marys and Our Fathers during recess. You can't imagine the ridicule to which I was subjected. I was a sensitive child. I begged him to relent, but not him.

TOBY: It would be nice to get even, wouldn't it, Louise?

(Prosecutor is about to object but Toby is quicker)

No further questions.

(Toby, Prosecutor, and Louise exit)

THE STUDY

MONSIGNOR: *(As he enters)* Father Rivard.

(Rivard turns to greet him)

After your extraordinary request, a Sister of Mercy living in the rectory, I thought it best I visit. I am most curious to discover why your question was ever asked.

PRIEST: But to come so far, and not even to let us prepare—

MONSIGNOR: Not far. The Bishop will consecrate the parish hall in Traverse City tonight. I have but one hour here. First, the Bishop wishes I speak with Sister Rita. Will you send your cook to the convent for her?

(Mrs. Shandig enters, hold hand up against sun, trying to see down the hill, then kneels and begins to "weed" her garden)

PRIEST: But, Monsignor, you see—

MONSIGNOR: Ah, Sister's teaching.

PRIEST: Yes, the school. She might be there.

MONSIGNOR: Then someone will watch her class.

(Sister Rita enters left and begins to help Mrs. Shandig in garden)

PRIEST: There are no classes on Saturday.

MONSIGNOR: Do you want me not to see Sister, Father Rivard?

PRIEST: Oh no. (Realizing Monsignor is still standing on front porch) Come in, Monsignor. I'll go myself.

MONSIGNOR: Perhaps there is something I might be reading in the meantime. For company.

PRIEST: I've finished three chapters.

MONSIGNOR: How many will there be, Father?

PRIEST: Seven.

MONSIGNOR: I see. One for each of the deadly sins.

PRIEST: Yes. Monday, Tuesday, Wednesday—

MONSIGNOR: *(As Priest hands him manuscript)* Am I to take it that this parish is not to your liking?

PRIEST: You'll see that the other four chapters are outlined in detail.

(Priest exits toward garden)

MRS. SHANDIG'S KITCHEN GARDEN

(Sister Rita and Mrs. Shandig are both "weeding" the garden on their hands and knees)

MRS. SHANDIG: Is someone visiting Father?

SISTER RITA: Everyone was here for confession this morning.

MRS. SHANDIG: It's that sun. All but makes you see things.

SISTER RITA: Imagine how it will be on the farms come harvest. They can't possibly carry water to the fields, just our gardens are more than enough to do.

MRS. SHANDIG: Sister. Those aren't weeds. They're new radishes.

SISTER RITA: I'm sorry. New ones.

MRS. SHANDIG: Sister. I never wanted you to move in because of the rule, but I like having you at the rectory. I do.

SISTER RITA: I do, too, Mrs. Shandig.

MRS. SHANDIG: Remember how you said you like radishes when they're sweet?

SISTER RITA: Yes.

MRS. SHANDIG: Well, I decided that I'd plant seeds every week, and you'd have the sweet baby ones right up 'til frost, Sister.

(Priest walks up to garden)

PRIEST: Sister, I have looked everywhere for—Monsignor Nicholson is here.

SISTER RITA: *(Starting to exit)* Oh no. Not when it looks so—I haven't dusted since Tuesday. Well, I can make tea, that won't take—

PRIEST: *(Stopping Mrs. Shandig)* Listen to me.

MRS. SHANDIG: What, Father?

PRIEST: *(Hesitating)* I'd rather . . .

SISTER RITA: What?

PRIEST: Well, I'd rather he not know that Sister lives in the rectory.

SISTER RITA: Doesn't he know already?

MRS. SHANDIG: Do you mean I should lie?

PRIEST: No. Not that. But everything short of lying. He, this Monsignor Nicholson, he, he's always looking for some mistake, some infringement, some mere interpretation that would prove that I am not capable to—

MRS. SHANDIG: *(Exiting)* Father, I'll help.

PRIEST: Come on then.

THE STUDY

(Priest and Sister Rita enter)

MONSIGNOR: *(Closing manuscript)* Pithy. Pithy, Father. Far more than I expected.

PRIEST: Why?

MONSIGNOR: Sister Rita. The Bishop sends you greetings.

SISTER RITA: Thank you, Monsignor.

MONSIGNOR: He is concerned for your well-being, Sister.

SISTER RITA: When the doctor comes to see the sisters, he talks with all of us.

MONSIGNOR: He wonders if we shouldn't consider closing the school, if it isn't—

SISTER RITA: But Father worked so hard to build it and—

MONSIGNOR: Yes. Yes. But until any danger of consumption—

(Mrs. Shandig enters with tea tray)

SISTER RITA: There's none. I'm not exposed to them.

MONSIGNOR: You're not?

MRS. SHANDIG: Sister doesn't sleep in the same room with them.

MONSIGNOR: You're the cook.

PRIEST: Mrs. Shandig, Monsignor.

MONSIGNOR: Yes. Where do you sleep, Sister?

MRS. SHANDIG: *(Pouring tea)* Sugar, Monsignor?

MONSIGNOR: Sister, I asked where you sleep since the other sisters—

SISTER RITA: Of course, I see them for prayers, but we are careful.

PRIEST: No sugar for me.

MONSIGNOR: Sister.

SISTER RITA: *(Starting simultaneously with Priest)* I go to mass in the church. They take the sacrament—

PRIEST: Have you any thoughts on my progress with the book?

(Mrs. Shandig hands Monsignor tea cup)

MONSIGNOR: No. And I don't have time for tea. Sister. I asked you a question.

PRIEST: At least, tell me, does the book look to be acceptable?

MONSIGNOR: Are you all hiding something from me?

(Silence)

SISTER RITA: I sleep in the convent of course. *(Looking to Priest for approval, then standing)* Will you come and see the school before you leave?

MONSIGNOR: Certainly. Thank you, Sister.

SISTER RITA: *(As they exit)* We are terribly pleased with what the children have accomplished.

(Sister Rita and Monsignor exit)

PRIEST: *(Throwing manuscript across room)* What have I done?

THE KITCHEN

MRS. SHANDIG: I'm stopping reading lessons.

SISTER RITA: *(Cleaning vegetables)* Why?

MRS. SHANDIG: I read good enough now for an older person. I'm not taking Thursdays off for a while. I'll do the cooking.

SISTER RITA: But that's the one day I cook. It gives you a little time for yourself.

MRS. SHANDIG: I just stay in my room, anyway. You cook too much, Sister.

SISTER RITA: Just Thursdays.

MRS. SHANDIG: *(Taking over cleaning vegetables)* No. Too much meat. I can't do anything with leftover meat on Friday.

SISTER RITA: Well, why didn't you tell me, Mrs. Shandig?

MRS. SHANDIG: I told Father.

SISTER RITA: He didn't tell me. He has not said a word to me the last week about anything.

MRS. SHANDIG: *(Trying not to cry)* He broke my bowl.

SISTER RITA: What do you mean?

MRS. SHANDIG: My good one. The blue glass fruit bowl. On purpose.

SISTER RITA: Why, Mrs. Shandig?

MRS. SHANDIG: (Crying) I don't know, Sister. Father's so strange. I'm worried. I told him about the leftover meat when you cook, and he banged the table so hard he knocked my bowl over.

SISTER RITA: What did he say about me?

(Priest enters, ignores Sister Rita)

PRIEST: Mrs. Shandig, I have to go over to Leland. I will not be back in time for dinner.

SISTER RITA: Father, I could wait up and cook you some—

PRIEST: (To Mrs. Shandig) I am speaking at the Grange. I believe they will serve supper there.

SISTER RITA: Why are you pretending that I'm not here?

PRIEST: Because as far as I am concerned you are not.

MRS. SHANDIG: (Rising, moving to exit) Father, would you excuse me? I have to feed the—

PRIEST: No. You stay. It was wrong of me to have Sister move in here. You were right, Mrs. Shandig. But I can't send Sister to Detroit now that she lied to Monsignor. They'd punish her so that—

SISTER RITA: But you were there. You could have corrected me, Father.

PRIEST: From now on, if you see me on the stairs, in the hall, anywhere, you will ignore it. As far as I am concerned you are back in the convent, and you will think the same. If it is ever necessary for me to speak to you, I will come to the school.

(*Priest leaves the kitchen*)

SISTER RITA: (*Calling after Priest*) Father, I only lied to Monsignor so that you wouldn't . . .

(*Mrs. Shandig exits left*)

THE PARLOR

(*Priest takes harness and sits. Sister Rita enters, watches Priest for a moment, then gets her scissors and brown wrapping paper. She waits in hopes Priest will speak. The wind outside and a ticking clock in the hall can be heard*)

SISTER RITA: (*Crossing toward Priest*) Father? A month. It's been a month since Monsignor visited. Four weeks, Father, and—

(*Silence as Priest continues polishing harness with vigor. She sits and watches. Mrs. Shandig enters with bowl of apples. Mrs. Shandig offers Priest apple, which he refuses. Mrs. Shandig sits and begins paring apples. Sister Rita seems frightened by silence, looks out window to valley, fights back tears of frustration. She begins noisily cutting a design in the brown wrapping paper. Eventually, the Priest throws down harness with annoyance. He takes missal from pocket and begins to read. Sister Rita, catching a look from the Priest, tries to cut more quietly, thereby making even more noise*)

MRS. SHANDIG: (*Unable to bear tension in the room*) What are you making?

SISTER RITA: Oh, for the school. Flowers. *(She holds up design)* I thought the younger children could paint them bright colors, and Louise could put them up with the compositions.

MRS. SHANDIG: *(Worried about Priest, trying to stop conversation)* I see.

SISTER RITA: There are so few flowers in the drought. The few in my garden will be gone by the weekend. Fridays I let them take little bouquets home. Everything so brown, these will be . . . *(Realizing no one is listening)* . . . nice. Nice.

(She tries to continue her work quietly, but aware Priest is more annoyed she takes paper and scissors and puts them away and then is unable to find anything to take her attention)

Would you like to resume the reading lessons after All Saints'?

PRIEST: I didn't know you had stopped, Mrs. Shandig.

MRS. SHANDIG: What's the use? There's no time. No time, Father.

SISTER RITA: We'll be all cooped up in here when it snows. Some days children can't even get up the hill they told me. By spring you could be a wonderful reader.

(Silence)

Why do you burn your lamp so late at night, Mrs. Shandig? It makes a square light on the ground.

MRS. SHANDIG: I hear you walking, Sister, so I work on the mending.

SISTER RITA: I didn't know you could hear me. I pray. Do you ever pray standing up?

MRS. SHANDIG: You must *walk* when you pray, too, Sister.

SISTER RITA: I'm sorry. I didn't know you could hear me. *(She waits for someone to speak, then looks out window)* I like to look at the few lights down in the valley, try to imagine why those three or four windows have a warm glow so late at night. Someone sick, a party, a student preparing for an exam, a baby being born. Do you ever do that?

(Silence)

Then I look at those trees behind the convent. Trees. They catch the stars, darken the ground. It's like you said, Father. I pray against the dark.

(Silence)

Do you know what I mean, Mrs. Shandig? About praying?

MRS. SHANDIG: I don't know, Sister. You are a nun. I never know what to say about such things. I don't stand when I pray. I didn't think you are supposed to. Are you, Father? I'm sorry. You want to read, don't you?

SISTER RITA: It is not disrespectful if you want to pray, Mrs. Shandig. God gave us a brain after all, and I think He expects us to use it.

MRS. SHANDIG: *(Rising, crossing to Priest)* Father, I wish Sister wouldn't talk personal like this. I don't understand things the way you do, Sister.

(Silence)

SISTER RITA: Well, you talk personal with the other sisters. I hear you, Mrs. Shandig.

MRS. SHANDIG: Not blasphemy, Sister.

PRIEST: *(Standing)* Mrs. Shandig. Let me talk to Sister. We'll say the rosary later.

MRS. SHANDIG: Yes, Father.

(Mrs. Shandig exits. Silence)

SISTER RITA: Can we, can't we just discuss it?

PRIEST: Don't you know we are very close to serious difficulty?

SISTER RITA: No. Why?

PRIEST: We cannot talk like this, Sister.

SISTER RITA: We cannot talk. We have not spoken a single word for a month.

PRIEST: Exactly as it should be, Sister.

SISTER RITA: No. I'm here, and you've got to let me help you. It's useless to stay locked in your study, striking out at poor Mrs. Shandig when all you need to— I don't live in the convent. I won't be ignored.

PRIEST: I want you to think what you've said.

(Silence)

Then you tell me. In the confessional. That is the appropriate place for you to speak to me.

SISTER RITA: Well, I suppose it all sounds especially Protestant to your particularly Catholic ears.

(She turns to exit, Priest grabs her)

PRIEST: Yes, it does. I sounds like, like . . .

(Silence. They face each other for a long moment)

SISTER RITA: *(Defeated)* I am trying to be a good nun, Father.

PRIEST: I know.

SISTER RITA: All of a sudden, this last month, nothing seems the way I . . . At Guardian Angel, we laughed all the time. And they held you if you cried. Here the sisters talk together in their beds. Then when I get there they have nothing to say to me, and yet they talk to Mrs. Shandig all the time.

PRIEST: You have the students.

SISTER RITA: Yes, Father. I do. I love watching them together, yelling and running down the hill. I almost hope they'll fall and scrape their knees so they'll come to me. That's awful. I didn't know it until I said— *(Stunned for a moment by her cruelty, then frightened)* I don't know what's wrong with me. If only I could talk things out, it would be so much better. Couldn't we have dinner together again? It's been so long since I ate with any—

PRIEST: We must accept God's Will.

SISTER RITA: It couldn't be God's will that we go out of our way to be unhappy.

PRIEST: One doesn't question God.

SISTER RITA: I never question God, only what men teach in His name.

PRIEST: Sometimes I think you want the Church to be imperfect.

SISTER RITA: I do not.

PRIEST: In Italy the peasants show their penitence by praying as they crawl on their knees up mountainous stone steps to the churches. They have been doing this for hundreds of years. By the time they reach the top the flesh on their legs is ripped, bleeding with small pieces of gravel imbedded in their skins. Bare bone shows through the men's best pants. And they don't complain. They don't snivel. They don't cry. They accept God and His Church. They smile at the top because they know God smiles. He is only satisfied when the pain of your prayers equals His in hearing our pitiful prayers.

SISTER RITA: Father, don't—

PRIEST: Don't pray when you're standing. Especially you shouldn't. It's not an appropriate gesture to God for you to make. If you kneel, it will remind you of your humility, your shame, and you'll stop questioning every—

SISTER RITA: Stop it. Stop. I can't stand this. I can't . . . *(Silence)* Have you ever been human? God is perfectly aware I respect and love Him, Father. And He knows I am human. Every breath I let out and every movement I make I try to make for Him. And if I felt closer to Him standing on my head when I pray, I would stand on my head.

PRIEST: Christ knelt.

(She slaps Priest. He slaps her)

SISTER RITA: How do I—I'm all alone. If there were just one thing about you that was human. I don't believe you have the same blood in your viens as I do. I don't believe it. Do you? Do you bleed when you're cut? There's nothing human about you.

(Priest grabs paring knife, jabs hand, holds it so she can see blood, then smears blood on Sister Rita's face)

PRIEST: Stay away from me.

(Mrs. Shandig, unaware of what has transpired, enters on the striking of the hour, carrying two rosaries. Sister Rita quickly wipes blood from her face as Priest takes handkerchief and wraps bleeding hand. Mrs. Shandig gives Priest his rosary. They kneel, each facing a separate way)

PRIEST, MRS. SHANDIG, and SISTER RITA: *(Crossing themselves)* In the Name of the Father, the Son and the . . .

Lights down.

Act II

Lights come up on Priest, Sister Rita, and Mrs. Shandig praying as they were at the end of Act I. They are saying the Lord's Prayer. When they reach "forgive us our trespasses . . . ," Rivard stands and calls out. Mrs. Shandig and Sister Rita silently complete the prayer.

THE CELL

RIVARD: *(Standing)* Guard, Guard. Can you hear me? Guard.

(Amos enters)

AMOS: Easy. Easy. You'll wake the whole damn town.

RIVARD: *(Crossing into cell)* How late is it?

AMOS: After ten-thirty. Is that all you wanted? I'll get you a clock tomorrow. Damn.

(Sister Rita and Mrs. Shandig exit)

RIVARD: Could you talk with me? For just a bit.

AMOS: Why?

RIVARD: I can't sleep. Sit down.

AMOS: So.

RIVARD: I suppose you've heard who the Prosecutor's calling next.

AMOS: Sure. Why?

RIVARD: You appear to be the kind of young man who knows what is happening.

AMOS: Erna Prindle. He's calling her.

RIVARD: Why Erna?

AMOS: Why he's desperate of course. He lost everything on Louise. Old Toby's really giving him a run for his money. Erna won't be able to say nothing. Maurice Prindle don't like you R.C.'s. He'll beat her black and blue if she lets on how she liked being a Catholic. Last year you should've seen her carrying trays over here with her arm broke. Wowie. Say, is it true, all that about nuns and priests?

RIVARD: What?

AMOS: Never have sex.

RIVARD: Oh. No, they don't.

AMOS: Really, Father? Really?

RIVARD: Amos, I imagine you could figure a way for me to talk with Erna.

AMOS: Sure. Why?

RIVARD: Before she testifies, I could—

AMOS: Oh no. No, Father. Ain't nobody can pull the wool over these eyes.

RIVARD: I want to comfort her, tell her not to stand up for me if Maurice would—

AMOS: Sure. And tell her what you want her to say. Pretend a confession or something and tell her what to do. I know about you R.C.'s. And, Father, I don't like it. Never did, even before the murder.

(Amos exits)

ERNA'S PARLOR

(Sister Rita enters. After a moment, Priest follows her. Silence, tension)

SISTER RITA: So this is Erna's. (Silence. After a moment, Sister Rita discovers a music box and begins playing it. Priest is startled and looks to see what the sound is) Music box.

(Priest turns off music box. Silence)

PRIEST: What you said last night. About me. It is not true.

SISTER RITA: I never should— I'm sorry, Father. It was just—

PRIEST: Let me say this before Erna comes back. Then it'll be over; you will forget last night. See, all this, it's your fault. And, and I need your help.

SISTER RITA: What is my fault?

PRIEST: I can't get done what I should. Here at Erna's I am to comfort her. This is a normal, routine matter for a priest. But I'm so confused that I know I need help. I have to if I'm to be a good priest. And I want to be. I must say what a good priest—

SISTER RITA: I never said you weren't a good priest.

PRIEST: Please, Sister. Hear me out. I can learn, or relearn. I can change. I have already, just saying out loud that I am afraid is a start. I have to tell you that Erna's mother, well, she is going to die. The doctor told me. And I thought all night about what you think of me, and very early this morning I decided that you should be here, that you would help me make a new start. I thought that if I hear you talk with Erna, I would hear the way you would try to—

SISTER RITA: You want mc to hclp?

PRIEST: Yes.

SISTER RITA: Thank you, Father.

(Erna enters. She has a handkerchief and is trying not to cry, but is barely succeeding)

ERNA: Mama's still sleeping. I checked.

SISTER RITA: My aunt's husband was sick something like your mother, Erna. The same. He stayed like your mother, just sleeping, for five days.

ERNA: But he died. Mama's not going to die.

SISTER RITA: But before. That was actually the hardest for me. I was terrified to be in his room, ashamed not to be.

ERNA: I'm afraid she'll hear me crying.

SISTER RITA: I know. I tried to keep it inside so my uncle wouldn't hear. Of course, he couldn't. I was much younger than you. I didn't know what was to become of me if he died.

PRIEST: Sister, maybe Erna wouldn't want to hear about this?

ERNA: Oh yes, Father. It's just the same. I have to be quiet too. And I don't know what'll happen either. I just don't. Mama and I, we take care of each other.

(Priest indicates Sister Rita may continue)

SISTER RITA: When I was in his room, I remember looking out the window. It was spring. I had just planted my garden. And there was a little sparrow at the feeder, but I'd forgotten to put out crumbs for worrying. Suddenly the sparrow flew down to the garden and started eating the seeds I'd planted.

ERNA: That's awful.

SISTER RITA: He was hungry. I wondered how he knew to do that. Whatever would make him know there were seeds there. Then I remembered that God watches over all things, even the sparrows. And, I thought, God will watch over me, too. I laughed. My aunt heard me laughing then.

ERNA: *(Crying openly)* Oh, Sister.

PRIEST: What Sister is saying is that God obviously was watching over her in her trouble. Just as He will watch over you and your mother, too, Erna.

SISTER RITA: And, of course, that is all I wanted to say, Father.

ERNA: Mama's not going to die, is she?

PRIEST: Your mother's lived a good life. She's a good Catholic. She has nothing to fear. You don't need to cry.

ERNA: No. No. No. Mama can't die.

PRIEST: Please, Erna. Listen to me. Crying won't help.

SISTER RITA: It can, Father. Just let her—

PRIEST: Erna, you must accept God's Will.

ERNA: I don't want to be all alone. She can't die. (*Throwing herself in Sister Rita's arms, crying*) What would happen to me out here? I'd be all alone.

PRIEST: Erna—

SISTER RITA: Father, perhaps, it would be better—

PRIEST: Your mother is in God's hands, isn't she? Don't cry, Erna.

ERNA: But I can't help it. When it starts, I just can't.

PRIEST: Pray for strength, say your rosary. "They who wait upon the Lord shall renew their strength. They shall mount up with wings as eagles, they shall run and not be weary." . . . See, if you try hard enough, you can resist the temptation to—

SISTER RITA: To be human? People have to cry, Father. Before you said that you—

PRIEST: Erna. Tears are personal destruction. Destruction of anything is an affront to God.

SISTER RITA: But Jesus wept. God was not affronted when His only begot—

PRIEST: Erna, you must accept all of God's world. Not just that which pleases you. Let me tell you a story of when I was a boy.

ERNA: Are you from Detroit, too, Father?

PRIEST: No. I came from a large family, very large. There were so many of us, in fact, that in order to feel important I told strangers I was an only child. But a real problem hit me and my family. Diphtheria.

In one winter I saw nine brothers and sisters buried. Also my father. After the first one, the baby, no amount of coaxing could get me to stop crying. Oh yes, I cried, Sister. I could not understand how God allowed such cruelty, those meaningless deaths. Why the baby? Papa? By Christmas I was the oldest brother. The house had been quarantined so I had to help. However, in the sick rooms, I just kept right on crying as if whoever I was serving was already dead. After a visit from me, mother would have to spend an hour in the sick room quieting the patient.

Even though we were forbidden to leave the yard, I had to get away. I thought if I ran hard enough and fast enough the tears would dry in my eyes and I would stop crying. I asked God to give me the strength not to cry. He didn't hear me. I sat by the river. I thought it was so useless that it would make no difference if I just relaxed and slid down the steep bank and let myself drown.

ERNA: No, Father.

PRIEST: I thought how can God let things be so bad. After all we know everything is God. He even allows evil so that we can confront it. And then I understood. Even the bad, the ugly, the cruel is part of God. To deny it, any part of it, is to deny God. I understood the world is evil and that unless I confronted it with strength I could never see the face of God. If you persist in believing only

in His goodness, then He casts you into everlasting—
(*Silence*) I stopped crying. I returned home and worked
hard, harder than even my mother. I went through the
crisis nights with a sister and then a brother, and the
doctor said I may have saved their lives. As soon as I
stopped crying, I became useful to God. I have not cried
since then.

ERNA: I don't mean to, Father. When it starts, I just
can't . . . I'm sorry.

SISTER RITA: Don't apologize.

PRIEST: No. She's right. Erna knows it's better to—

SISTER RITA: People don't apologize for crying, for
feeling. Erna only needs—

PRIEST: (*Standing to leave*) Sister, this is not the time
to discuss—

ERNA: Oh, no, not yet. Don't. Please don't, Father. I'll
get the coffee and the muffins. They're the kind you like.

(*Erna exits. Long silence*)

PRIEST: You should not have spoken as you did in
front of Erna.

SISTER RITA: You asked me to help you, Father.

PRIEST: You made her cry. Erna is hopeless without
the strength and the reason to control—

SISTER RITA: She does not have to be a saint.

PRIEST: You leave this place. She does not. She has got
to have control.

SISTER RITA: She's not crying because she's selfish.

She's crying because she's scared. Erna needs to believe she won't be left all alone. That's all she needs.

PRIEST: The Church does not exist to meet every sniveling need people have.

SISTER RITA: The Church does not despise people and what they do.

PRIEST: While you are in my charge, you will never question me again.

(The sound of the church bell calling people to confession is heard. Sister Rita kneels as Priest puts on confession stole)

THE CONFESSIONAL

SISTER RITA: Bless me, Father, for I have sinned. It has been one week since my last confession.

PRIEST: *(Simultaneously) In Nomine Patris et Filii et Spiriti Sancti.*

SISTER RITA: Father, ever since we went out to Erna's farm, I've been trying to understand what I did wrong.

PRIEST: My child, do you think you might have been presumptuous?

SISTER RITA: Yes. Every week I confess that imperfection. But there must be more that I should confess.

PRIEST: No. That is all, Sister.

SISTER RITA: Then why do you act like I've—

PRIEST: How do I act? This is the confessional.

SISTER RITA: But this is my only chance, Father.

PRIEST: You talk to God here. Only God. Do you hear me?

SISTER RITA: Father Rivard gets so angry with me, God. I don't know why. I don't know what he expects of me. I don't know what I do that makes him—

PRIEST: (*Standing*) No. I'm not hearing it the way I should.

SISTER RITA: It's my confession.

PRIEST: I don't have the proper attitude of distance.

SISTER RITA: (*As Priest leaves confessional*) You can't stop my confession. I have to confess. What will happen? I can't go to Communion.

THE COURTROOM

(*Erna is in witness chair about to be examined by Prosecutor. Rivard sits with Toby*)

PROSECUTOR: Did Father Rivard say a novena after your mother's death?

ERNA: Yes. To St. Jude.

PROSECUTOR: Who is this saint, St. Jude?

ERNA: The patron of hopeless and desperate causes.

PROSECUTOR: Hopeless. Desperate.

ERNA: He said we both needed strength.

PROSECUTOR: The priest needed strength because he was hopeless and desperate.

TOBY: Objection. The Prosecutor is not only leading the witness, he is—

PROSECUTOR: I withdraw the question. Erna, why—

ERNA: For mama. For mama. The novena was for mama. He didn't pray for himself. He prayed for everyone. That's what they do.

PROSECUTOR: Erna. Please. Erna, only answer my questions. If just thinking about novenas is upsetting, we'll talk about something else. Why did you stop being a Catholic?

ERNA: I'm a born Catholic.

PROSECUTOR: In what church were you married?

ERNA: Can't we talk about something else?

PROSECUTOR: Mrs. Prindle, in which church choir do you sing?

ERNA: I'm a Methodist. But I am Catholic, too. (*To Rivard*) I'm raising up the children Catholic as much as can be, Father. I'm teaching them the rosary.

(*Erna puts hands over mouth, shocked at her slip*)

PROSECUTOR: Maurice's children know the rosary.

ERNA: No. No.

PROSECUTOR: Does your husband, Maurice, know about rosaries in the house?

RIVARD: Leave her alone.

(Rivard starts to stand, but Toby stops him)

ERNA: It wasn't wrong to marry him. Maurice is a good
man. No other priest ever came to Holy Rosary after Father left.

PROSECUTOR: So that was reason enough to desert—

ERNA: I didn't know what to do.

PROSECUTOR: Erna, how can we understand that a
good Catholic girl, who knows all about novenas and
saints and heaven knows what, a girl who teaches her
Protestant children secretly the rosary . . . how can we
understand that she would marry outside the Church?

ERNA: But Sister said there was no reason—

PROSECUTOR: Sister Rita.

ERNA: Yes.

PROSECUTOR: Told you to marry a Methodist.

ERNA: No. No, you don't know how it was.

PROSECUTOR: How was it then, Erna?

ERNA: After mama died, I was teaching Sister some
handwork. On the day of the fire, I came in and brought
her some jonquil bulbs and to work with her, and she
told me it was all right to go to the Methodist socials.
That's all.

PROSECUTOR: To look for a husband?

ERNA: There weren't any unmarried men who were
Catholics.

PROSECUTOR: And you hooked Maurice, right?

ERNA: No. No, it wasn't like that.

PROSECUTOR: Erna, as a former Catholic, would you expect a good nun to encourage a mixed marriage?

RIVARD: Make him stop.

(*Toby quiets Rivard*)

ERNA: I'm still Catholic, and Sister was a good—

PROSECUTOR: Not Sister Rita. Any nun. Does a good nun break the Church rules? Yes or no?

ERNA: No.

PROSECUTOR: Yet Sister Rita wanted you to marry a Methodist.

ERNA: I was all alone. She only told me I could go there to the socials. I didn't know what to do. I was all alone out on the farm. There were sounds at night. Sounds I never heard before. And I was going to be an old maid. I'm not very pretty, you know. I'm not. You don't know. I had to do what I could. Father? Father?

(*Erna stands, holds arms out to Rivard, but is held back by Amos*)

RIVARD: (*Standing, starting toward Erna, held back by Toby*) Leave her alone. Leave her alone. This cruelty must stop.

(*Erna sits*)

PROSECUTOR: If the defendant wishes to make a statement he must be under oath.

TOBY: Objection.

RIVARD: Now. Not after the verdict. Now.

PROSECUTOR: I want this in the record.

RIVARD: Listen to me. I was there, but I didn't help.

(Silence, as he crosses to comfort Erna)

TOBY: I move this court be adjourned until such time—

(Following spoken quickly and overlapping)

RIVARD: Enough cruelty has happened.

TOBY: This is inadmissable.

RIVARD: This cruelty must not happen because of me.

PROSECUTOR: I want this in the record.

RIVARD: No, don't. I'm innocent of all that.

TOBY: Rivard.

RIVARD: I know I was wrong.

TOBY: He's not under oath. This doesn't count.

RIVARD: But he is destroying these people who've come to help me.

PROSECUTOR: Everything I'm doing is to get to the bottom of the crime.

(Toby takes Rivard to seat)

RIVARD: *(Lunging at Prosecutor)* Everything I did was for the Church. He is trying to destroy Erna.

(Rivard punches Prosecutor in stomach. Amos grabs Rivard)

TOBY: Take him out. Amos, take him.

(Amos takes Rivard to cell)

PROSECUTOR: *(Exiting)* I will call no more witnesses. The Prosecution rests.

(Amos throws Rivard into cell where Sister Rita is waiting)

SISTER RITA'S GARDEN

(Sister Rita, wearing a shawl to war off autumn cold, sits on ground, tatting and singing "The Lilac Song." He walks to her, enjoys watching her)

SISTER RITA: *(Singing)*
     Spring brings promises in the lilacs,
     Dreams of lavendar and green.
     When I hide myself in lilacs,
     Winter's sadness seems a dream.
     The scent of the lilacs like a gentle wind;
     The touch of the flowers like a baby's hand.
     Oh lilac, you can grow when the earth is cold.
     You are here when no one knows.

PRIEST: You sound happy. *(Sister Rita continues singing)* I've come here to your garden many times. Just to think. I will miss it this winter.

SISTER RITA: So will I.

PRIEST: Did you watch the sunrise?

(Silence)

SISTER RITA: I don't want to detain you.

PRIEST: I have time. This is a bit of a celebration today. In a sense. You see I am finished with the book. Forever.

SISTER RITA: You did; it's . . . I'm so used to you being busy, Father.

PRIEST: What are you thinking?

SISTER RITA: (*Continuing her tatting*) The lilacs will survive the drought. Maurice told me. He's going to give me some lilacs from behind his shop next spring.

PRIEST: How is it that you talked to Maurice?

SISTER RITA: He let me go with him to Traverse City.

PRIEST: When? I didn't give you permission.

SISTER RITA: I have to go there for confession.

(*Silence*)

PRIEST: What are you doing?

SISTER RITA: Tatting. Erna taught me.

PRIEST: You don't think you spend too much time outside the Church, do you?

SISTER RITA: Father, I took responsibility for my well-being a month ago at confession. Helping Erna does not interfere with my teaching or other responsibilities. Erna and I are friends. I think I understand her. She feels quite unloved, useless without her mother.

PRIEST: Sister, I am only concerned that you might waste time—

SISTER RITA: (*Standing, preparing to leave*) I intend to waste even more time on Erna. I don't really care what you do or think.

PRIEST: Please. Don't talk like that.

SISTER RITA: I know what it's like for Erna day after day. Night after night. Those dreadful stripes on my bedroom wall. It's like a prison. I can't sleep. I can't breathe. I have to get out and walk in the hall up there.

PRIEST: The same wallpaper is all through the house. In my room, too. *(Silence)* Let Erna go to the Methodist socials.

SISTER RITA: What do you mean, Father?

PRIEST: Let her go. Maybe you shouldn't say that I am allowing it. Otherwise, everyone in the parish—

SISTER RITA: Thank you, Father. I'll tell her. Thank you. *(Putting her hand on his arm)* I can't even say how I feel. That you're helping Erna. That you finished your book. That maybe now you'll have time for—that we could—that you'll bring me that lilac bush from the valley you promised. *(They laughed)* I, I'd like to read your book.

PRIEST: I destroyed it.

SISTER RITA: What?

PRIEST: I'll never leave here. I burned it.

SISTER RITA: Why, Father?

PRIEST: Well. I thought I knew God. God, the Vengeful. The God of Job. That God, He was the one I set out to write about. Then you came, and I tried to fit into what I know the things you said, the things you— It wasn't possible. I don't know God now.

SISTER RITA: Father, your life work. To destroy it.

PRIEST: Sister, I am fit for nothing more than this small parish. If this. And I will have to fight to be worthy of this.

SISTER RITA: I couldn't have said anything so bad that you'd destroy it because of me.

PRIEST: Because of, or for you. What difference does it make? Maybe God is only hope. Why else do you and I keep promising each other such senseless hopes? No one ever gets what he works for, what he wants. That's God's order. See, I didn't know that before you came. You taught me.

SISTER RITA: Oh no, no, no. Every night. I've had this conversation a hundred times. Every night I couldn't sleep. I expected it all differently.

PRIEST: What else did you expect?

SISTER RITA: I don't know. I don't know.

(Sister Rita exits. Toby enters)

THE CELL

TOBY: Listen, you son of a bitch, what are you doing to me?

RIVARD: What? What do you mean?

TOBY: Standing up, talking like some crazy man in the court.

RIVARD: It was for Ema.

TOBY: Rivard. Look, you know I never argued an actual trial before. Not like this. Hell, I never even cross-examined a witness before.

RIVARD: You've done it well.

TOBY: I know. But, Rivard, I need your help. I can't do

it alone and on top of everything I've found out you lied to me.

RIVARD: I never lied to you.

TOBY: *(Taking letter from pocket)* There was a light up at Holy Rosary very late last night, just like there used to be. I went up. I found this.

(Rivard paces)

"Bishop, I beg that you transfer Sister Rita. I know now I shall never leave this place. Sister does live in the rectory. I made her lie to the Monsignor for my own selfish reasons. Sister has a way about her, and it makes me think I am loving her. I know I must run from this temptation, and I do, but I grow very weary. Very weary." You wrote it, but you didn't mail it.

RIVARD: But I wrote it the last day. It was too late.

TOBY: Too late for what?

RIVARD: Please stop. I don't want to remember anymore.

TOBY: Then change your plea. It'll be easier for you, and I do not know what else to do. See, then I could probably get it down to second degree.

RIVARD: Murder.

TOBY: Reduce the charge. Second-degree murder. Second degree would be the most they could give you, and as a matter of fact—

RIVARD: No. She's dead. There are no degrees in death.

TOBY: But they won't hang you. That's what matters, isn't it?

RIVARD: No. It's not. Please. I don't care if I live or die. I just want to remain insane.

TOBY: *(Taking a small whiskey flask from his pocket)* You're sane. You proved that standing up in court. Asking for some room there to be left over for common human decency. And when you did that you put a rope right around your neck.

(He takes a swallow. Rivard refuses the offered whiskey)

At least you're saner than the crazies up here. They drink and spit, plant and wait, sit and stare. After a while the pupils in their eyes seem to enlarge so that all they can see clearly are gravestones, and two-headed calves, and the wounds of the horses which they themselves back into unseen equipment. They are past care, so I argue their deeds and wills, travel to Leland to see lantern slides of European castles, and wonder how men lost the ability to dream and accomplish. And I fish. Mainly I fish. But you, Rivard, you make me wonder about what a man might do. They shouldn't hang you. It'd pleasure them more than they deserve. See, I didn't care much about you, one way or the other, when I first saw you. But I care 'cause I s'pose I know that you're a tad like me. And I figure you're worth saving. 'Course maybe now I'm just madder than them. I want to help you. I think I can. Let me change your plea so you can live.

RIVARD: I can't do that.

TOBY: I hope you can bear up then. 'Cause somehow I'm going to find out 'bout that last night. The night of the fire.

RIVARD: All right, counselor. We have to.

(Rivard reaches for whiskey. Smiles. Takes a deep swallow)

TOBY: They still haven't found Shandig. Some hunters said they saw a woman living out in an old, deserted loggers' camp last fall. Maybe that's her. I know she's still in the area 'cause she comes into Solon a couple of times every year. She trades muskrat skins. Now I'm thinking she might be back up at Holy Rosary. Somebody's there. Lights on. House all cleaned up, and your cassock was laying out on the bed. Yes. Mrs. Shandig expects you back, Rivard. That's for sure. *(Starting to exit)* Yeah, I'm going up there.

RIVARD: *(To Toby)* I tried to save Sister. I did try to save her.

(Toby exits. Fire alarm bells ring. Stage is flooded in the light of a fire. Sister Rita appears upstage in silhouette. Priest takes off jacket. Sister Rita runs to cell. She is wearing a street dress)

SISTER RITA: *(Calling as she runs, looking everywhere for Priest)* Father. Father.

FRONT PORCH

SISTER RITA: *(Afraid to touch him, but needing to)* Mrs. Shandig told me you were hurt in town fighting the fire.

PRIEST: It's only my leg. It's a bit hard to stand. I couldn't run well enough if the fire turned so I came back up.

SISTER RITA: Maurice said the town is saved, but the farmlands will burn to the bay. The fire almost reached Holy Rosary, but they stopped it by digging a fire ditch.

PRIEST: What are you wearing?

SISTER RITA: I had to put it on. Down in the town. There were all those flying cinders. My robe caught fire.

PRIEST: Are you hurt?

SISTER RITA: No. It's Sophie's mother's.

PRIEST: (Sitting) Aren't you tired? I'm so tired. I think that must be why I fell and twisted—

SISTER RITA: (Kneeling beside him, wiping dirt from his forehead) I was so afraid— There's dirt all over you.

PRIEST: (Taking her hand from his face) Please. You shouldn't be out of your habit. When we're so tired, you shouldn't be out of your habit. Go inside and change.

SISTER RITA: It's only us. Everyone else is down there. I have this feeling. And it's us. I know it's only us. What is it? It's not knowing that hurts so much. If I could understand, if I could, then it would be all right again. I could do what is right. But I don't know. Please help.

PRIEST: The Bishop will help. I wrote him today. I asked that you be transferred.

SISTER RITA: No, not that. I'll never know.

PRIEST: We don't want to.

SISTER RITA: I want to. All my life I'll wonder.

PRIEST: No. You'll forget. Go upstairs. Now.

SISTER RITA: How could I . . . how could I be so wrong?

PRIEST: (Standing) Don't do this.

SISTER RITA: I felt this, and . . . I wish I'd die.

PRIEST: Go up. Pray.

SISTER RITA: I can't.

PRIEST: Save us.

(Sister Rita runs inside. Priest kneels to pray)

PRIEST: Holy Mother, hear me. Precious Jesus. God.
Am I in Your Image? God, make me strong. I doubt. I
doubt everything. "They who wait upon the Lord shall
renew their strength." I am waiting, God. I have always
waited. Help me. God.

*(Priest abruptly enters rectory when he hears Sister Rita's
cry, which overlaps his prayer)*

SISTER RITA'S ROOM

SISTER RITA: *(At window)* Where is my garden? The
fire ditch. They dug the fire ditch right through my garden. All the bulbs are dug up. The roses. They burned.

(Priest holds her until sobbing subsides)

PRIEST: At night I wonder how you are feeling, what
you think, if you're happy, if you can sleep. Even when I
pray, I wonder what you're doing. I look up through a
window if it's recess or I listen for your steps in the hall.
I can only concentrate if I pray about you. Almost to
you.

(He is about to kiss her)

SISTER RITA: Please. Tell me what it is.

PRIEST: I have. *(Silence)* I love you.

(They kiss)

SISTER RITA: I never dared think—I thought, who else would have me but the Church? But with you I'm not nothing, am I?

PRIEST: No. You're not.

SISTER RITA: I'm just like everyone else.

PRIEST: *(Pointing to page in diary)* What's that?

SISTER RITA: Just my diary. I always keep it in the drawer. *(Starting to put it away, then stopping)* But it's all right now, isn't it? *(Handing it to Priest, a gift)* Do you want to read it?

PRIEST: It's drawings.

SISTER RITA: Not all of it.

(She sits with Priest to look at diary)

PRIEST: No. Of course not. This can't be Sister Immaculata, can it?

SISTER RITA: I think she must have been in a grump that day.

PRIEST: Every day. Did you show her this?

SISTER RITA: No one's ever seen it. I offered to show it to Mother Vincent, but she said the only sin it could possibly be is boring.

PRIEST: She was wrong. This is so easy. Why was I so stupid? I don't understand why it seemed so worthy to—

SISTER RITA: Why do we have to understand? Has trying to understand been so wonderful?

PRIEST: No.

SISTER RITA: *(Pointing to page in diary)* Who's that?

PRIEST: Me? Well, you sure got the eyelashes. *(Pause)* You make me so happy. And you made me so miserable.

SISTER RITA: I never meant to. *(Leading Priest to window, still holding diary, eager to share)* Look. Where I stood all those nights. See. We can be with all the other people now. We aren't so different after all, are we? Don't look at the Church. Look down there with the other families. We'll be like that, too.

PRIEST: We can't move down there.

SISTER RITA: We'll have our own children.

PRIEST: Children.

SISTER RITA: Oh yes. I should have known. Oh, all those nights. Known that if the Church wasn't everything, that you would give me something in its place. I think somewhere inside I always knew I was not a true Bride of Christ.

PRIEST: You thought of this before.

SISTER RITA: No. Just the confusion. In there you'll see. I just didn't know.

PRIEST: What did you write?

SISTER RITA: It doesn't matter, does it?

PRIEST: Read it to me.

SISTER RITA: Someday, whenever, you can read it all—

PRIEST: Read it to me. Now. Read it.

SISTER RITA: *(Looking as she sits in front of window)* Well, any page these last few weeks. "I think Father

Rivard must be right. Maybe the Church is only for rules, but God is for people. According to the rules, everything I feel is wrong, yet nothing feels wrong. Do I have a conscience? Yes, I do. Do I belong in the Church? I don't know. He makes me so confused."

PRIEST: We can never lose our faith.

SISTER RITA: We won't.

PRIEST: We can't even think of it.

SISTER RITA: *(Standing)* Now look. The lights are going on in their homes. We can think of that. We'll be down there and then—

(Priest suddenly pulls her from window)

What is it?

PRIEST: Mrs. Shandig is coming up the hill.

SISTER RITA: But we can tell her. Everyone.

PRIEST: No.

SISTER RITA: Why?

PRIEST: *(Moving to exit)* Because I, I—I'm their priest. She depends on me. They all do. I'm the only way they have of understanding.

SISTER RITA: People understand.

(She crosses to stop his exit. He grabs her by the arms)

PRIEST: It's not how you think it is. Their homes have photographs of babies in coffins. Adolescents pour kerosene on kittens, and their fathers laugh when they set the fire. Sometimes wives cannot cook breakfast. Their fingers are broken from their husband's beatings. It's only because they think I'm different; it's only because they think I'm worthy that I can help them. I must be worthy.

SISTER RITA: *(Putting arms around his neck)* I think you're worthy. Please. You said you loved me. I know you're too good, too precious to escape, desert me when—

PRIEST: I'm not, not what you think. I, I, I've destroyed all that. For the Church. *(Pushing her onto stool)* There's nothing left for you. I can't be a husband. I can't be a father. There's nothing left but cruelty. That's all I know. That's all I worship. All I need. Not the resurrection, life. It's the nails. My salvation. Only the agony. There's no chance for—

SISTER RITA: You're not cruel. It'll be different now.

PRIEST: Damn you. Trying to break me down, make me forget. *(Taking her head in his hands, forcing her to look out window)* Planting those flowers out there as if you, you could make the world beautiful. What makes you think you could change anything? Promising me things will be better. You make them worse. It's not my fault you lost your faith. It's not. You never had any if it dies so easily.

(He starts to rip up diary. She wrestles it from him)

SISTER RITA: No. That was before. You can stop. That's gone. It's gone.

PRIEST: *(Pushing her from himself with violence)* With them, with them, I can make it look all right. They only want me to say those words. They don't want to know me. You can't know me. I'll destroy you. You can't know me. You'd hate me. I hate myself.

SISTER RITA: I don't hate you. God doesn't hate you.

PRIEST: *(Trying to exit)* Don't talk about God.

SISTER RITA: *(Holding him from exit)* We still have God.

PRIEST: I don't want God. I don't want you. *(Starting to choke her)* I hate God. I hate God. I want to kill God. I always wanted to kill—

(He drops Sister Rita on floor. For a moment, he thinks he has killed her. He pulls her to a sitting position, slaps her on the back. She coughs. He gets wet cloth, sits next to her, wiping her brow)

SISTER RITA: *(As she stops choking)* I'm sorry. I'm sorry. What you said. Hating God. It's my fault too. You couldn't—

PRIEST: No. No. It's me. •

(Mrs. Shandig enters)

SISTER RITA: We have to help each other. It's all we have now. We only have each other.

MRS. SHANDIG: *(Moving to Sister Rita)* Sister. What are you saying?

SISTER RITA: Please. Mrs. Shandig. Leave us alone.

MRS. SHANDIG: What is wrong? What you said . . .

(Sister Rita crying throws herself into Mrs. Shandig's arms for comfort)

SISTER RITA: Tell her. Please tell her.

MRS. SHANDIG: Tell me what.

SISTER RITA: Tell her.

MRS. SHANDIG: Tell me what.

SISTER RITA: *(Turning from embrace to Priest)* Just tell her, and it will be over. Please. Tell her you love me.

MRS. SHANDIG: *(Crying)* Sister. No. No.

PRIEST: You haven't done anything. It's just me. There'll be a train. I'll walk to Traverse City. The fire didn't affect the trains there.

SISTER RITA: I'll go with you.

PRIEST: No.

MRS. SHANDIG: Father, you can't go.

SISTER RITA: *(Suddenly embracing Priest)* Don't leave me. I don't care if I go to hell.

MRS. SHANDIG: *(Pulling Sister Rita from Priest)* Father, you hear her. *(About to hit Sister Rita)* Don't touch him.

PRIEST: *(Catching Mrs. Shandig's hand)* Stop it. *(To Sister Rita)* I won't hurt you anymore. You can leave. But you must leave the right way, when your community tells you. Go back to your order.

SISTER RITA: I'm not a nun now. I'm nothing.

PRIEST: There's still a place for you. They need you.

SISTER RITA: I haven't even said it to you.

PRIEST: Don't say anything. Don't think it. Honor your vows. It's the only way. The rest is me. I cause it. God isn't cruel.

SISTER RITA: *(Crying, hitting Priest)* No. No. No.

There's nothing left. *(As Priest leaves)* But I never told you. You never heard the words. Let me tell you.

(Sister Rita crosses to window to watch Priest walk down hill)

THE COURTROOM

MRS. SHANDIG: *(In witness chair)* Father walked down the hill. Sister watched from her window 'til he was almost out of sight, and then she screamed after him.

SISTER RITA: I love you.

MRS. SHANDIG: He didn't even hear her.

(Sister Rita exits. Toby walks to Mrs. Shandig. Amos and Prosecutor enter)

TOBY: Now I want to understand this clearly, Mrs. Shandig.

MRS. SHANDIG: Yes, sir.

TOBY: When she called to him, he did not turn back.

MRS. SHANDIG: No, sir. He's a priest.

TOBY: He did not return that night.

MRS. SHANDIG: No, sir. Never. I thought he would, and now he has.

TOBY: Did anyone else, anyone come up the hill that night?

MRS. SHANDIG: Maurice came up.

TOBY: What did he do?

MRS. SHANDIG: He planted a small lilac bush from the town. He told me Father paid him to do it.

TOBY: Did Maurice see Sister Rita?

MRS. SHANDIG: I don't know.

TOBY: Now, think. Did Sister see Maurice?

MRS. SHANDIG: Sister went to her garden. She saw the lilac. She touched it, just like she was always touching things and then she went all crazy. She threw herself down on the ground, crying and sort of rolling back and rolling back and forth. She rolled herself right into the ditch they'd dug to stop the fire and she didn't get up. She just lay there in the ditch shaking, like deep sobbing, staring up at me with dead eyes.

TOBY: I see. I see what you mean. Then what did you do?

MRS. SHANDIG: I prayed to St. Jude for strength and guidance. He answered my prayer, because I understood the lilac was a sign from Father. He paid Maurice to plant the lilac as a sign to me to bury her in the garden. She was too evil to put in the cemetery. (*Quietly, without emotion as she explains the absolute logic of her action*) I looked at her down there like a snake. She was laying there just like a dead snake. I know that look. When I was a girl I had a snake. My mother saw me playing with it. She took a hatchet and ran into the yard and chopped it all up. It kept wiggling after it was dead. All the pieces moved. I didn't know then that they kept moving until the sun set. She was wiggling down there and making noises, but it was near on to the moonrise, so I knew she was dead. I went to get the shovel. I scraped the dirt back into the fire ditch over her dead wiggling body. I was nearly finished when the dirt over her started to rise. The earth didn't want her body, but I hit the snake's head and shoveled the dirt faster on its face and then it was peaceful. The moon came up and Holy Rosary was silvery and white again, and the fire was far, far away.

TOBY: I move this case be dismissed on the grounds that the People's case cannot support a verdict of guilty beyond a reasonable doubt.

(*Mrs. Shandig looks at Rivard for some sign of approval. He looks away, and Amos crosses to Mrs. Shandig with his handcuffs clearly in sight. She looks at Amos confused. He gently leads her to exit. Prosecutor follows to exit*)

GRAVESIDE

(*There is the distant, haunting sound of a train whistle. A lialc bush in full bloom is seen where the cell was. Rivard is standing by lilac. Toby walks over to join Rivard*)

TOBY: Rivard. Whew. This hill's too much for me. (*Silence*) So this is, is where Sister Rita was buried.

RIVARD: Yes.

TOBY: Rivard. I have to tell you. (*Silence*) Mrs. Shandig, she killed herself at the jail. Banged her head against the wall till she was dead.

RIVARD: No, no. It will not stop.

TOBY: (*Touching Rivard's shoulder*) I'm sorry. Oh, sorry I called Shandig, and sorry I thought I was so damned clever. At least you can have forgiveness in your Church, can't you?

RIVARD: Not unless you know God. She gave me a chance. Will I never see the Face of God?

TOBY: What are you planning you'll do, Rivard?

RIVARD: What are you going to do?

TOBY: Fish. Mainly I fish.

RIVARD: Mourn her. Mainly I'll mourn her.

(Rivard reaches to touch lilac. Toby steps back several steps, his head bowed. Rivard kneels.

Sister Rita enters. Rivard looks up into her face. He cries. Toby takes a step forward, but waits)

Lights down.

Night Rainbows
an afterword

Afterwords are nice. You aren't expected to read them.
Introductions—and prefaces even more so—demand to
be read first. Introductions, for books such as this one, frequently seem to be written by the likes of Harold Clurman
or Eric Bentley, who seriously put into context (bury) that
which has yet to be experience (read). And, thereby, give
away many of the plot's surprises.

Prefaces, of course, appear mainly before plays by
George Bernard Shaw, who so painfully puts the unread
into such a difficult context that the unread often remains
unread. But afterwords, like P.S.'s to letters, don't really
count, except in such critical cases as "P.S. And if you
don't return the keys, I will change the locks."

So . . . some afterwords about representative first words
from the women who sparked the play, and selected production words from the producers and directors who
brought it to life. . . .

I

My mother died in the fall of 1964. Not all at once
though.

My estranged wife and I united briefly in Detroit to
watch Mama under plastic, perfectly preserved, with the

tubes connected to the machines hired to do the last of her living. Our unity was short-lived. My sensible wife hurried off to buy me a pair of black shoes at J. L. Hudson's. Obviously I couldn't wear desert boots to the funeral.

Sometimes Mama's hand would involuntarily brush the hair off her forehead. It was a habit I knew well. She'd always done it just as she was about to wake from a nap on the davenport. Standing there in the hospital, I would ready myself to apologize when she woke, to promise I'd go back with my wife, to vow anything if Mama would just smile again.

The last time I'd seen Mama conscious, she was crying, because I had announced the separation from my wife. "After all I've done for you, how can you do this to me? If you'd just give up show business and smoking, and come back to Detroit, none of this divorce business would be necessary."

Her cerebral hemorrhage had been massive. And I wouldn't ever see her smile.

At the moment I heard of Mama's fatal attack, I had remembered an English professor once saying in an Oresteia lecture, ". . . and, of course, the greatest crime is matricide." I thought, well, now I will know. I stood by the bed waiting to experience the Furies.

* * * * *

At the funeral, I believe I was the only one who didn't cry. But I was uncomfortable; my new shoes pinched something awful.

Returning to New Haven, I tried a reconciliation with my wife in a new apartment, and at Yale I avoided John Gassner's eyes when he said that there was still one playwright who had not turned in an outline for his full-length play. A full-length had to be completed acceptably by May, or the playwright in question would be dropped by Yale. It was already October.

My wife attempted to cement our reunion by giving me an idea for a play. A play about a trial which took place near her hometown in Michigan many years before she was born.

According to what she had been told, a priest had been tried for the murder of a nun. At the last minute, his housekeeper had confessed to the murder on the witness stand, but everyone knew she was only protecting the killer-priest whom she loved.

I thought it was a lousy idea. Melodramatic. No, she said. She herself had once thought of writing a play based on the trial; and, therefore, it was not a lousy idea. Her plan had been to have the story through a series of prayers, both ritual and personal. That, I said, was even a lousier idea, because it would result in an undramatic melodrama.

Except I kept wondering: How could a crime of passion happen in a rectory, a place of such intense containment? It would be some years before I would realize that the crime was due precisely to that containment.

Gassner accepted the outline for *The Guilty*. I planned to make the priest legally innocent, not a killer. Then in the twist ending, it would be revealed that he was morally guilty. I changed the story as my wife had related it so that the priest would leave the nun alone with the housekeeper, even though the housekeeper would have already confessed to the priest her plan to kill the nun. He would, of course, be honor-bound throughout the trial not to reveal the confession, and I could have a justifiable, well-made, last-minute revelation. In the denouement the priest would declare: "I am guilty. If I had left her alone with a lion, the lion wouldn't be guilty. I would be. And I am."

I had a secret goal I set myself. I wanted to move the audience to tears, to make them empathize with a man who could not cry, even when he was guilty for the death of a loved one.

* * * * *

In writing the first draft, every experience seemed pertinent to the play. For example, when working on character names, I met the head usher at the Shubert, Mr. Shandig.

At Yale, Professor Prouty had explained an Elizabethan metaphor: night rainbows. "Don't you see? It's like 'hot ice.' There can't be rainbows at night." I immediately thought the night-rainbow metaphor conveyed the essence of the nun's pain. So I added a line in their first meeting so that the priest could tell Sister Rita that the Indians had called Solon the Land of Rainbows, an attractive image which would help make her love the place all the more. But then, late in the play, as the nights lengthened and her isolation was increasing, she could plead to the priest, "But there can't be rainbows at night."

A friend told me an experience from his childhood that I felt belonged in the priest's childhood. The priest would tell it in the dining room scene, although later I moved it to the scene where he and Sister Rita attempt to comfort Erna.

Let me tell you a story of when I was a boy, Erna. Where I grew up, everything was lawn and cobblestones and sidewalks. Therefore, there were very few pebbles or stones. So that is what I collected. All little boys collect what they think is rare. So I collected rocks.

One day I was walking home from school. I found a sandstone. It wasn't valuable, but a special color. Some bigger boys saw me looking at the stone and told me to give it to them. I didn't want to because I'd found it. I suppose they only wanted it because I held it so tightly. So I ran. They were right after me. You run faster when you're scared.

I ran into the house and closed the door. They stayed outside. Calling my name over and over. My married brother asked them what was wrong. They said I'd taken something of theirs. A rock. He believed them. Without even asking me, he pushed me back outside and locked the door so I couldn't get back in.

After the boys were through, I ran. Nowhere in particular, just ran. I thought if I ran hard enough and fast enough the tears would dry in my eyes, and no one would know I was crying. I asked God to give me the strength not to cry. I prayed very hard. And it worked. He heard me. I have never cried since then.

I thought the story represented the essential injustice of childhood that can confuse, warp many adult lives. Since the play in that draft was to be principally about justice, the story would also enhance my main theme. The story suggested a "running" image which I thought might make for a more poetic title. The play was renamed *Run So Fast the Tears Dry in Your Eyes*. (Well, that *was* the year we were all looking forward to *The Persecution and Assassination of Jean-Paul Marat as Performed by the Inmates of the Asylum of Charenton Under the Direction of the Marquis de Sade*.)

My marriage disintegrated further as the play grew, and I was so involved in the play that I even avoided discussing our difficulties when my wife wanted to. I would have trouble writing if I were emotionally upset by an argument or a threatening discussion. So, for the most part, we stopped talking. Even touching. Even in crowded elevators. But somehow, somehow I felt that if we could stay married, then Mama wasn't so dead. And in that, I found comfort in marriage. However, we finally talked to the only conclusion, divorce; and I finished the play on schedule.

II

John Gassner recommended the play to an important New York agent. "This play could go on Broadway," the agent said. "But it could take you ten years of rewrites to pull it together. You'll need time to write such grown-up themes."

Intending to decimate my agent's time schedule with the amazing maturity of my final rewrite, I returned to Yale ready to revise on the basis of her suggestions. Fellow student Arvin Brown liked the new version, and wanted to direct the play for his final project, providing I rewrote it so that everything that happened in the play happened in the priest's mind. Since the play was too long, Arvin's idea gave me a principle not only for rewriting, but also for cutting. By the time I finished the rewrite, Arvin had left Yale in order to work as the children's theatre director at the Long Wharf Theatre.

* * * * *

After graduation, I, too, went to work at the Long Wharf as special projects director. An apprentice and Catholic, Irene Walsh, read the play for me to check the accuracy of my Catholic references. What I expected, her love and admiration, was not forthcoming.

"Sister Rita couldn't live in the rectory; nuns live in convents." "But it was a small parish," I argued. "It doesn't matter. There's no way she'd be sent 500 miles to live with the priest." "Well, it's a true story, and that is the way it happened." "I don't believe it, and I don't think other Catholics will either." It had never occurred to me that the nun could not live with the priest, and, of course, I knew nothing about the actual situation. "Also I can't believe any priest could be so aloof from his parishioners."

I rewrote the play to win Irene's approval. I thought that putting the church on a hill would help define the priest's attitude. To make Sister Rita's living in the rectory more acceptable, I invented two other nuns and infected them with tuberculosis so that they would not have to appear in the play. The nun would then have to move to the rectory to avoid contamination.

Irene reread the play at the end of the summer and found it believable. Well, at least, bearable.

* * * * *

When my agent said Richard Barr wanted to see me, I was certain the long wait, the rewrites were nearly over. I bought a new tie and dug out the seldom-worn good black funeral shoes. They still pinched. But I didn't want to appear casual, indifferent in tee shirt and desert boots.

Barr thought the play too much of a character study. "Enhance the excitement. Increase the courtroom drama. Maybe go back to Michigan, read the actual transcript."

I'd named Solon after the county in which the real town, Isadore, was located. Solon means lawgiver, and back in the early days of a play exclusively about justice that made sense.

I was surprised to discover that Isadore was built in the center of a flat terrain, with only one hill on which sits the

Catholic Church. Aside from television antennas and a paved road, the town looked exactly as I had described it.

The night before my visit the rectory had been struck by lightning and stood gutted, blackened. The priest had been forced, therefore, to move temporarily into the convent. I was able to explore the old rectory to my heart's content.

I didn't stay long.

Although blackened by fire, the entire house, every single room, was papered in stripes, exactly as I had imagined it.

The first thing I read in the transcript was that the nun had been brought to Isadore to help since the other sisters had consumption. Then I discovered that I had somehow managed to write six lines of testimony for my Erna Prindle that miraculously duplicated, word for word, six sentences of recorded testimony. The last thing I read was the housekeeper's confession. She believed that as she testified her hair was turning into snakes.

If ever there were a time that I was convinced that I was "chosen," that I was not presumptuous to be a writer, it was during the seven-hour drive back to my father's apartment in Detroit. I just kept thinking, "I really know how people feel. How people act. What they say."

Probably it was some vestigial superstition that prompted me to go back to my childhood Methodist Church that Sunday. The text was Isaiah XL:21: "They that wait upon the Lord shall renew their strength; they shall mount up with wings as eagles: they shall run, and not be weary."

I decided to call the Barr rewrite *But the Runner Stumbles*. That much the trip helped.

The transcript encouraged me by its similarities, but since the housekeeper had been the one tried, the priest not even being present, the truth wasn't going to help me. (I thought it was curious that the Protestants had changed the story so that not only was it the priest they believed to have been tried, but they even thought he was in fact guilty.) It took more than a year to write a version I did not really believe in, but Barr was my only concrete hope.

"I'm afraid I don't like this approach any better, and I suspect your original inclination was the right one," Barr said.

I set out to rewrite, returning to my original concept, but maintaining a new character from the Barr version, the lawyer Toby Felker.

More potential directors and producers.

More rewrites.

III

As director Pirie MacDonald and I worked on the script in preparation for a summer 1971 production in the Boston University Playwrights Project at the Berkshire Theatre Festival, he kept coming back to the Mrs. Shandig-as-lion metaphor at the end of the play. The use of an exotic animal metaphor in turn-of-the-century Michigan did not seem organic, especially since it was so abruptly introduced at the end of the play. The official Michigan state animal is a wolverine, but I couldn't do anything with that, so I justified the lion image by working circus metaphors into the play, even adding a scene in which the nun and priest took the students to see a travelling circus. Finally, during the Stockbridge rehearsals, I couldn't bear the phony circus talk and accepted that my first instinct on the lion image was wrong.

We cut the lines.

The play worked fairly well, and word drifted back to New York and other words drifted to Stockbridge. David Merrick's office would option the show if I would add a nude scene for the nun and priest. Alexander Cohen's representative suggested an option if, through a rewrite of the priest, I could make the play a vehicle for Robert Preston. Two young company managers saw the play pretty much the same as I did and optioned it for Broadway. Unfortunately, after two years and two more rewrites, they could not raise the money.

* * * * *

An actor-writer friend, Joseph Mathewson, gave the script to Alfred Goldfield, board president of Manhattan Theatre Club, and also to Austin Pendleton, the actor-director. Austin liked the play, and simultaneously the Manhattan Theatre Club decided to do it.

At the Cincinnati Playhouse-in-the-Park, where Austin was playing Tartuffe, we worked on a rewrite in which we attempted to clarify the priest's character. Trying to define Rivard's relationship to the Church, I wrote the "in Italy the peasants" speech during the first act. Austin came offstage for intermission, read the new speech, liked it, and then played the second act.

Well into rehearsals, Austin asked me to do something about the priest's rock story: "It's so long, and it really doesn't accomplish anything. At the most it'll get just some kind of 'Awww-poor-boy' reaction." And again I argued that such a reaction was precisely the purpose of the story. Since the theme of the play was no longer justice, I had no argument on those grounds. "The priest is a difficult man for the audience to get into," I maintained. "They need some point of identification to get inside him. That's what the story accomplishes."

Austin was patient. "Okay, okay," he said. "I buy that. But if the audience hasn't gotten into the priest by the second act, we're in deep trouble."

That night I wrote the diphtheria story, and we put it into the show the next day. It worked better, even in a first reading. It evoked more than pity, we thought, and also helped fill in information about his childhood and explain the priest's strange devotion to his cruel God.

Every actress who has ever read or played Mrs. Shandig has wanted to play insanity. Sloane Shelton was no exception. I told Austin that Sloane was playing the snake speech all wrong, nearly rolling her eyes in the madness. The terror for the audience has to come from the cold logic of the speech, I explained. Even though it does not quite make specific sense, Mrs. Shandig does not know this. She is attempting to explain clearly to the lawyer what transpired. And, most of all, she wants the priest to understand what a splendid thing she has done. Sloane steadily simplified the speech in Stamford and again on Broadway until ultimately Mrs. Shandig's madness was distilled into a simple unconscious gesture at the end of the speech, which often caused audiences to gasp.

The production was running about two and a half hours, and every night at the post-play discussions Austin and I

heard from the audience that the play was too long. Austin
and I, along with the cast members, would then go to
Hasting's for dinner and talk cuts.

The nun's speech by the window near the end of Act I
seemed to evoke program rustling, which we knew was certainly not to be blamed on Nancy Donohue's performance.
It was necessary to keep the section in which the nun en-
joyed her fantasies about the lights in the valley homes in
order to help prepare for her rapid transition later from
nun-hood to hopes of motherhood. However, her extrava-
gantly poetic description of Solon's desolation was implicit
in other scenes. We cut most of the description, maintaining only "trees, catch the stars" and the climactic line,
which I refused to cut, "Solon's not a Land of Rainbows at
night; there can't be rainbows at night." I argued for the
retention because of preparation for the last line of the
play, which was said by the priest to the nun: "Don't you
remember, Sister, there can't be rainbows at night?" That
line was our current attempt at an ending which would reveal some growth for the priest, something for the play beyond a final absolute despair.

The last scene at Manhattan Theatre Club was not
working. No one laughed, but no one cried as I intended.
Austin and I decided to try a scene in which the Monsignor would return to Solon and offer Rivard a job at the
Guardian Angel orphanage and convent. This would be
sad, but still enough of a projection, enough of an upbeat
to end the play successfully. It worked better, but was not
wholly satisfactory yet.

Since the new scene eliminated the romantic and rather
indulgent last line about "rainbows at night," I could not
justify the earlier rainbow line for the nun. Even though
we had a go at trying it in the Erna's Farm and the Sister
Rita's Garden scenes. But it was no go.

Manhattan Theatre Club's executive director, Lynne
Meadow, requested Actors' Equity to allow us to extend
our run beyond the absurd twelve performances Equity
permits Off Off Broadway.

The last performance in the extended run was seen by
Margot and Del Tenney, who wanted the play for their ini-
tial season at the Hartman Theatre Company, in Stam-

ford, Connecticut. Based on our Manhattan Theatre Club experience, we worked on a new version, this time in a Boston theatre dressing room where Austin was standing by for Joel Grey in *Goodtime Charlie*. We decided that we should show more scenes that were described in testimony, such as Rivard's banishment to Solon by the Monsignor.

IV

On December 3, 1975, at 7:50 A.M., I was already sitting on the 8:05 to Stamford. I had not slept well anticipating the first day of rehearsals. As always, I had again been visited by the nightmares that had come every time *Runner* was rehearsed. Mama kept trying to tell me something. I could never understand what it was.

Austin sat down opposite me and read the newest rewrites as we reverse-commuted with all the Haitian maids on their way to make the beds of Connecticut.

Austin had never been keen on the title *The Runner Stumbles* and had even asked his acting students at the Berghof Studio what they thought. They loved the title, and Austin said he was finally growing to like it himself.

As soon as we arrived at the Hartman Theatre, I rewrote the one page Austin had not liked, typed it and xeroxed it before the actors arrived. As I passed out the new pages, Sloane Shelton quickly checked the changes, then belligerently asked, "Where's my song? Milan, you promised me a number. I'm not even in the dream ballet anymore." I gave Sloane a set of pencils personalized with the name Mrs. Shandig on them, and she was happy. As were the other actors with theirs.

The reading went well. The new ending Austin had approved on the train ("Mainly I'll mourn her") sounded right! The play was a bit long, but Austin and I knew how to cut by then if nothing else. I'd slipped the "rainbows at night" line back into the script. When it was read Austin smiled, made a mark in his text, and I knew he'd found the first cut.

Our rehearsal space in the old Palace Theatre's second

floor lobby was so cold that most days I had to do the rehearsal rewrites with gloves on.

* * * * *

Just as we were about to dash for the train to New York, Hartman producer Del Tenney caught Austin and me. He explained that the program and poster printing deadlines were the next day. He was concerned with what smart-ass critics would do with the title: "Last night the Runner Stumbled at the Hartman."

Austin and his wife, Katina, rode the train with Sloane and me. Austin and I were exhausted. We kept looking through the script for titles, each suggestion making us laugh harder than the last. *Babies in Coffins. Mainly I Fish. Rainbows at Night.* (I didn't laugh at that one.) Katina was determined we call it *Erna's Farm.* Sloane picked a legal expression from a trial scene: *Privileged Communications.* I was surprised that Sloane's usual zany sense of humor had deserted her. Then I realized she was serious. Then we were all serious. Austin loved it. Every scene had to do with communication. It was one of the important themes to us.

I checked the title out with two friends to whom I constantly turn for criticism, Gray Boone, a *Runner* investor, and Martin Lee Koslow, Spanish translator of *Runner.* They were long-acquainted with *The Runner Stumbles* and loved it, but concurred that as long as I felt the change useful, it was okay. They also shared my feeling that *Privileged Communications* somehow sounded familiar. However, The Theatre Collection of The New York Public Library reported no record of a play ever being so named, and a call to the Library of Congress did not turn up such a title, even for a novel.

Del Tenney liked the new title, but in the final decision-making meeting, Margot Tenney pointed out that critics could twist the new title just as well: "*Privileged Communications* should have been kept privileged." We tried the Devious Critic Test on other titles. "*Our Town* sure isn't mine." "*Much Ado About Nothing* certainly is." "*The Birds* is exactly what this comedy is for."

We kept my title.

* * * * *

The blocking rehearsal, when the director tells the actors where to move and when and why, always fascinates me. Especially with Austin, because no question or comment is too small or inconsequential for him to ignore. Everything is discussed, and yet the whole play is blocked in a day. Therefore, I was startled by his brusk response to a suggestion of mine ("I'll fix that later"). I was concerned that he had left the priest frozen in a past-tense scene while the courtroom proceedings continued. If the play was written so that its focus always emanated from Father Rivard's mind, what would the audience think when the priest was ignoring the proceedings?

I returned somewhat crestfallen to the stage manager's table and consoled myself by joking with the stage manager. An unfortunate choice because the stage manager was trying desperately to transcribe the blocking. My timing seemed to be off with everyone.

Later in the morning Austin directed the priest to help move a table during a courtroom scene so that it would be placed correctly for the subsequent dinner scene in the priest's house. "Austin, if the priest doesn't think the trial is important enough to watch," I asked, "why should the audience?" Austin threw his script on the floor. "Then if he can't do that, I don't understand the play, and can't stage it at all. Everything I'm doing is wrong."

He called a lunch break. Neither of us ate. We stood on the stage discussing calmly, rationally every piece of blocking. But neither of us was making any sense in our frustration with the other's stupidity by the time the actors began floating back to rehearse. We made an obvious show for them of how everything between us was patched up.

I was told I mumbled all night in my sleep, "Austin, it won't work. I can't do it."

We met on the train to go over some cuts I had been working on but avoided any talk of staging. The walk up Atlantic Street from the train to the theatre was bitter cold and silent. Suddenly, Austin said, "I hate that shitty staging. What are we going to do?"

I wanted to hug him, but instead talked about the importance of keeping the audience focus directed through the priest's mind. At the theatre he began moving the miniature furniture on the set model trying to find a better ground plan. His mind flew. Within five minutes he had a new concept, and the set designer was concerned about the adjustments. Austin explained, "The priest must be the focal point of all scenes."

Wayne Adams saw one of our first rocky performances. He called my agent from the Stamford train station. He wanted to bring the production to New York even though his prior producing experience was limited to a college tour of *Jacques Brel Is Alive and Well* . . . and of Off Off Broadway production of *The Homecoming*. We suggested that he and his partner, Willard Morgan, wait to read Clive Barnes' *New York Times* review. "I don't care if Barnes hates it. This play has to be fully realized in its appropriate space." (What "full realization" meant was never quite defined, but Austin and I ultimately learned it meant: exactly what you've got . . . only better . . . and shorter . . . and truer . . . but mainly better.)

I had expected the Stamford production would finally move me to tears, but it didn't. However, Clive Barnes thought we had "one of the best first plays in a long time. It got to me and I cried." His tears provoked an even more emotional flood of Broadway production offers. "How would you like Albert Finney and Diana Rigg?" For a new *American* play? We went with Wayne Adams and Willard Morgan, who were willing to risk bringing in the non-star cast which we had carefully rehearsed and worked with for over a year.

V

My sister Susan and I were sitting with Gray Boone and Martin Lee Koslow in my living room on the afternoon of the Broadway opening. As always, my friends were discussing what I should wear. We were happy, and I said, "It would be perfect if Mama could be here tonight to see—" And I cried. I could not stop.

The show opened twelve years after I first put pen to legal pad. Two years later than my first agent had predicted. That agent wasn't at the opening. She does not handle plays anymore. In 1968 she announced she would handle only screenplays because "Broadway's too slow."

I paced in the back of the balcony during the opening performance. I wore desert boots.

Chelsea, New York City
September, 1976